Teacher's Resource

ImpactEnglish

MIKE GOULD, KIM RICHARDSON, MARY GREEN & JOHN MANNION

Key Stage 3 – Year 7 • Teacher's Resource 1

William Collins' dream of knowledge for all began with the publication of his first book in 1819. A self-educated mill worker, he not only enriched millions of lives, but also founded a flourishing publishing house. Today, staying true to this spirit, Collins books are packed with inspiration, innovation and practical expertise. They place you at the centre of a world of possibility and give you exactly what you need to explore it.

Collins. Do more.

Published by Collins
An imprint of HarperCollins*Publishers*
77–85 Fulham Palace Road
Hammersmith
London
W6 8JB

Browse the complete Collins catalogue at
www.collinseducation.com

© HarperCollins*Publishers* Limited 2005

10 9 8 7 6 5 4 3 2 1

ISBN 0 00 719512 5

Mike Gould, Mary Green, John Mannion and Kim Richardson assert their moral rights to be identified as the authors of this work

All rights reserved. No part of this publication may be reproduced, stored in a retrieval system, or transmitted in any form or by any means, electronic, mechanical, photocopying, recording or otherwise, without the prior written permission of the Publisher or a licence permitting restricted copying in the United Kingdom issued by the Copyright Licensing Agency Ltd., 90 Tottenham Court Road, London W1T 4LP.

British Library Cataloguing in Publication Data

A Catalogue record for this book is available from the British Library.

Acknowledgements
The following permissions to reproduce material are gratefully acknowledged:

Text: Extract from *Harold, Bella, Jammy and Me* by Robert Leeson (Heineman Ltd.), p9; extract from *Computers for Beginners* reproduced from by permission of Usborne Publishing, 83–85 Saffron Hill, London EC1N 8RT, UK. Distributed in the USA by EDC Publishing. Copyright © 1997 Usborne Publishing Ltd, p17; extract from *Gulliver's Travels* by Jonathan Swift, p26; extract from 'The Science of Superheroes' from BBC Science & Nature at bbc.co.uk/sn, p31; extract from ONLY YOU CAN SAVE MANKIND by Terry Pratchett published by Doubleday. Used by permission of the Random House Group Limited, p47; extract from *Two Weeks with the Queen: Play* by Mary Morris, based on the novel by Morris Gleitzman (Macmillan Children's Books, 1994), pp72–73; 'Bournemouth in the rain' © Bill Bryson. Extracted from NOTES FROM A SMALL ISLAND by Bill Bryson, published by Black Swan, a division of Transworld Publishers. All rights reserved, p97; Blackpool Sea Life Centre advert reproduced with permission, p105; extract from 'Pen pal dangers' from *mizz*, 17 April 2002, p113; extract from *The Rime of the Ancient Mariner* by Samuel Taylor Coleridge, p125; 'Sample Two' extracted from 'Triumph and despair: Haile Gebrselassie' by Jamie Jackson from *The Observer*, 1 June 2003 © Jamie Jackson, p150.

Images: Alasdair Bright, NB Illustration: pp25, 54.

Whilst every effort has been made both to contact the copyright holders and to give exact credit lines, this has not proved possible in every case.

Printed and bound by Martins the Printers, Berwick-upon-Tweed.

Page layout by Ken Vail Graphic Design, Cambridge

Cover design by ABA-design, Ascot

Contents

Introduction		4
Peer Assessment Sheet		6
Unit 1	Terror in the night	8
Unit 2	Myths and legends	24
Unit 3	Out of this world	40
Unit 4	A life of crime	56
Unit 5	Drama in the making	72
Unit 6	Far from home	88
Unit 7	Media today	104
Unit 8	Past lives	120
Unit 9	Sporting challenge	136

Introduction

The following icons are used:

 In pairs   Test watch

 In groups   Extra resources

The Impact English Teacher's Resource is designed to provide a comprehensive set of resources to aid your teaching, based on the units in the Student Book. In essence, the Teacher's Resource consists of dedicated teaching plans, worksheets, OHTs and assessment materials, designed to help you make an impact on students' learning and progression.

Structure

Each unit in the Student Book consists of three key source texts and an extended Assignment. In the Teacher's Resource we provide:

Source Texts and Tasks

For each of the 27 source texts and sets of activities:
- 2 lesson plans (each with **Starter**, **Introductory work**, **Development** and **Plenary**)
- 2 support resources (OHTs, worksheets, etc.)

These are all cross-referenced to **Framework Objectives** (also referenced in the Student Book).

Extended Assignments

For each of the 9 extended Assignments:
- 1 lesson plan
- 1 planning or support resource (worksheet or OHT)
- 1 OHT showing sample responses at the current and targeted NC levels.

Each of the lesson plans for the Assignments is targeted at one or more of the **Key Stage 3 Assessment Focuses**.

Assessment practice

A full practice test and advice, based on the optional and main English **Key Stage 3 tests**, as well as a comprehensive mark scheme, are available to download from www.collinseducation.com.

Using the materials

Whilst you can, of course, use the lesson plans and support materials in their entirety, the resources are designed so that if you choose only to teach one unit or one text from the Student Book you can do so.

The Framework Model

The lesson plans have been devised around the Framework lesson model, and particular care has been given to make the Plenary session active and meaningful and not simply a recap of what has been taught.

Peer Assessment

A key element of the lesson plans for the Assignment is a Peer Assessment section. In this, the students have the opportunity to measure the drafted work against pre-set criteria and then have their work evaluated using the **Peer Assessment Sheet** on page 6.

Differentiation

For each of the three Student Books for each year, there are individual Teacher's Resources. While the base material is the same, the lesson plans and resources have been significantly adapted and changed to meet the different levels and skills needs of the students. Thus, worksheets and OHTs have different levels of demand, or are, in some cases, entirely different. In a similar way, some Starter activities and Plenaries focus on entirely different areas, appropriate to the students' levels. Finally, the Assignments are designed to move students up different levels so the teaching materials are adapted accordingly.

CDs

All lesson plans and support resources are contained on the accompanying CD-Rom as Word files, so they can be customised further according to the needs of your students.

Interactive whiteboard resources and assessment exercises are also available separately on the *Impact English Whiteboard Resources* CD-Rom.

Finally…

All in all, the *Impact English Teacher's Resource* provides you with a vast range of lesson ideas, support resources, assessment opportunities and back-up. Whether you use it as a flexible, 'dip-in' resource, or as a complete taught programme, it should act as a major stimulus on your students' learning, and assist you with your planning and resource provision.

Peer Assessment Sheet

Name: ....

Date: ....

Class: ....

The assignment involved writing a...

Which main text-type features were included in the writing?

What were the good points about the writing?

What needs to be improved?

Writing overview (for you or your teacher to complete)

FOCUS	Poor	Average	Good	V Good
Sentence structure and punctuation (the way your sentences are put together; the accuracy and effect of your use of punctuation)				
Text structure and organisation (the way your writing is organised; for example, whether your paragraphs help the reader to follow what you want to say)				
Composition and effect (the particular choices of words and phrases used to fit the sort of text you are writing) plus how well you interest the reader.				

ImpactEnglish Year 7

Lesson plans and resources

For use with Impact English Year 7 Student Book 1

A horror story

Terror in the night

Lesson 1

Framework Objective

R2: Use appropriate reading strategies to extract particular information (scanning)

Main text type: Narrative

Student Book pages 4–8

Starter

- Discuss the conventional narrative pattern (i.e. beginning, middle, end) that is typical of traditional stories such as folk tales. Introduce students to the idea that this pattern can be altered, pointing to examples such as television drama, that involve cliffhangers or time shifts. Tell students that the story they are about to hear is unconventional, but say no more.

Introduction

- Ask students to imagine they are reading the story from the actual *More Horowitz Horror* collection. Refer to the glossary definition before reading the story to the class.

Key Reading

- Before discussing the text type, ensure students have grasped the gist of the story (which is crucial when they come to scan the text later on). Run through the key feature of narrative texts, as shown in the text-type box, focusing on the crisis and the story ending. Check understanding by asking these questions:
  – Do you think the crisis will ever happen? Say why or why not.
  – Why does the reader have an important part to play in the story?
- Make sure that students understand that they have a part to play in the story as readers by finding the hidden message and working out the ending (see question **1**). Discuss question **2** as a class.

Development

Purpose

- Use questions **3** and **4** as the focus for a group discussion.

Reading for meaning

- In order to solve the message in the story, students must scan the text to locate the correct letters. Use the example given to demonstrate how to do this, then ask students to complete question **5**. When the message has been solved, refer back to questions **3** and **4** to discuss the story ending and the writer's intention in light of the new information. Students then scan the text for further information in question **6**.

Plenary

- Pull together the main points of the lesson:
  – key features of narrative texts
  – how authors can play with these for effect (for example, the highpoint and the ending)
  – the usefulness of scanning.
- Ask students to complete **Worksheet 1.1** to reinforce their scanning skills.

Unit 1 Terror in the night

Worksheet 1.1: Jammy

Read this text and the questions below it. Then scan the text to find the answers and underline them in red.

> We had four in our gang in Tarcroft, Jammy and Harold and Bella and me. Jammy's real name was Alan but we never called him anything else but Jammy. Why? Because whatever he did turned out right – for him. He always had jam on it, so we called him Jammy.
>
> Don't ask me how he did it. Some people are made like that. He was so lucky it was sickening. He was cheeky with it too. But I liked him, he was a good mate.
>
> And bets – he always won bets. Never bet with Jammy, we always said. He's too jammy. But we always ended up taking him on. The odds were so tempting.
>
> This day we were out bike riding. Well, we were out with our bikes. We had two bikes between us. Jammy had an old cronk which his Dad had found somewhere and fixed up. The frame must have been made for a six-year-old and the saddle was raised so high Jammy looked like a circus performer perched up in the air.

From *Harold, Bella, Jammy and Me* by Robert Leeson

1 What was Jammy's real name?
2 Why was he called Jammy?
3 Where did the gang live?
4 Name a girl member of the gang.
5 How many bikes did the gang have?

A horror story

Terror in the night

Lesson 2

Framework Objectives

S11: Vary the structure of sentences within paragraphs to lend pace, variety and emphasis

Wr5: Structure a story with a satisfying resolution

Main text type: Narrative

Student Book pages 8–10

Starter

- Ask students to think of examples of exciting stories or films. Point to tales of horror or thrillers, encouraging the class to recognise that 'surprise' is a key ingredient that keeps the reader's attention. Remind them that surprise can also be a feature of a story ending, producing a 'twist in the tale' – a feature of *The Shortest Horror Story Ever Written*.

Introduction

Focus on: Story endings

- Follow the Starter with question **7**. Most students should recognise what is happening in the illustrations, but ask them:
  - *What is happening in the first illustration?*
  - *Who is unaware of what is to follow in the second illustration?*
  - *What do the captions tell us?*
- Reinforce the idea that the 'twist' suggests the story has not ended yet. Use this to lead into a discussion of cliffhangers and how they create suspense, making reference to TV soap operas which are familiar to most of the class and which regularly use this feature.
- Read the example with the students and ask them to imagine the scene. Then ask them to discuss, in groups, several possible outcomes of the cliffhanger and to report back to the class.
- List their suggestions on the board and help them create complex sentences to complete the cliffhanger by writing up some examples. Then refer back to the Student Book to illustrate how sentence structure can be varied to retain the reader's interest. Use the example given and, if possible, the students' own sentences. Students can attempt question **8** on their own. **Worksheet 1.2** can also be used for extra support and could be given as homework.

Development

Key Writing

- Students should now be ready to attempt writing their own cliffhanger (question **9**). Supply useful verbs for less able students; for example, *shuddered, quivered, trembled, grabbed, wrapped* (these should also suggest possible nouns). Emphasise that students should vary their sentences to create interest.

Plenary

- Ask 2 or 3 students to read their story endings. The class should decide whether these create tension or suspense. Recap on the main points related to story endings with twists and cliffhangers, and emphasise the need for sentence variety in students' writing.

Unit 1 — Terror in the night

Worksheet 1.2: Vary your sentences

We can vary our sentences to make them more interesting. For example:

- *It slipped out of the open window, without looking back.*
- ***Without looking back**, it slipped out of the open window.*

The following paragraph is uninteresting because all the sentences begin the same way, with the pronoun 'it'.

***It** stopped and raised its head, sniffing the air. **It** looked around. **It** slithered across the floor, leaving a trail of slime. **It** made its way towards the far side of the room, swiftly. **It** clambered up the wall, with a huge effort.*

1. Choose three sentences from the example above to change round. Use the commas as a guide.
2. Cross out the sentences you are going to change.
3. Write the new sentences underneath.
4. Read the paragraph again. It should sound more interesting.

Terror in the night

Lesson 3

Framework Objective

R14: Recognise how writers' language choices can enhance meaning (repetition, line length)

Main text type: Poetry

Student Book pages 11–16

Starter

- Explain that poets make patterns with words, and that poetry comes in many forms. Ask students to think of some examples (they may be familiar with shape poems, for instance). Point out that one of the ways in which poetry is distinguished from prose is that it is written in lines, not sentences. Demonstrate this by referring to a novel and a poem.

Introduction

- Students may assume that the two main types of poems are those that rhyme and those that have no rhyme. Explain that, in practice, a lot of free verse contains rhyme, and that it is the irregular rhythm that is significant. Draw students' attention to the difference between the irregular beat in free verse and poetry with a regular beat, using **OHT 1.3** to illustrate this. *Oranges and Lemons* has an obvious regular beat and rhyme. The free verse poem *Evacuees* has an irregular beat, and also contains rhyme. Ask students to tap out the beat of each poem to demonstrate this. Also reinforce the way in which both poems are written in lines.

Key Reading

- Read the poem to the students and then go through the key features of poems in the text-type box. Check understanding by asking these questions:
  - *Can you give an example of rhyme?*
  - *What is another word for rhythm? How is it different from rhyme?*
- Go through questions **1**, **2** and **3** and establish that *Big Fears* is a free verse poem with an irregular rhythm.

Development

Purpose

- Use question **4** to lead into a discussion of the rational and irrational nature of fear, as expressed in the poem, asking for students' own examples.

Reading for meaning

- Questions **5**, **6** and **7** explore 'writing in lines' and the way this differs from sentences. Make sure that students can hear the difference. Point to the example from *Big Fears* to emphasise how sound effects can be created when words are dropped, and encourage students to recognise that meaning can be accentuated.
- Students can work alone with question **6**. They will need to experiment with writing lines in different ways until they create something they like. This work will be used again in **Lesson 4**.

Plenary

- Elicit from the class the main points of the lesson:
  - poetry is written in lines not sentences
  - you can hear the difference between prose and poetry as well as see it
  - free verse has an irregular rhythm.
- Finish by asking students to explain the difference between rhythm and rhyme.

Unit 1 — Terror in the night

OHT 1.3: Rhythm and rhyme

Read these two poems and then answer the questions below.

> *Oranges and lemons*
> *Say the bells of St Clement's.*
> *You owe me five farthings,*
> *Say the bells of St Martin's.*
> *When will you pay me?*
> *Say the bells of Old Bailey.*
> *When I grow rich,*
> *Say the bells of Shoreditch.*

Traditional poem

During the Second World War many city children were sent to the countryside to escape the bombing. They were called 'evacuees'.

```
The label pinned to my red winter mac
Says who I am,
As if I might forget my name.
And rooted to the spot,
I stand and stare,
At all the labelled children,
In coloured coats and scarves and hats,
Like presents wrapped,
Waiting for the mail train.
```

From *The Evacuees*
by Mary Green

1 Which poem has a regular beat or rhythm?

2 Which poem rhymes? Look carefully!

Big fears

Terror in the night

Lesson 4

> **Framework Objectives**
> **Wr3:** Use writing to explore and develop ideas (brainstorming)
> **Wr8:** Experiment with the sound effects of language (rhythm)
> **Main text type:** Poetry

Student Book pages 16–18

📖 Thesauruses should be available. Students will also need work completed in **Lesson 3**.

Starter

- Demonstrate to students how punctuation can emphasise meaning. For example, the dash acts like a pause but can also add emphasis, as in:
   He was on time – for a change.
   Commas indicate a pause in a sentence, but they can also be used to change meaning. For example:
   John claimed Peter broke the window. John, claimed Peter, broke the window.

Introduction

Focus on: Punctuation and repetition

- Explain that punctuation in poetry can also help to create meaning. Refer to the example on page 14 of the Student Book, discussing in particular how the pause in the final line helps to alert us to the possibility of something sinister happening – the opposite of what the line actually says. Read the line to the class, demonstrating this effect. Then ask the students to answer question **8** in groups, reading the line in a variety of ways to change the meaning and using the comma to help them do this. Ask them to feed back their examples.

Development

- The use of repetition in *Big Fears* is a way of giving a poem a form or frame. Follow the Student Book example and work through question **9**, drawing attention to the capital letters in the line. Then, using the line as a model, ask the class to create new lines about fear that could be used for repetition. You can begin this activity as a brainstorming exercise: think of a key word (for example, *ghost*) and brainstorm for associated words (for example, *wraith, spectre, phantom*). Encourage students to use thesauruses.

Key Writing

- Students can now call on the starter lines they wrote for question **6**, and the repeating lines from the brainstorming session above, to write their free-verse poems, for question **10**. Encourage them to use punctuation (for example, *commas, dashes*) to emphasise meaning. They should also try to hear the rhythm of their lines, as this will produce more successful poems. Less able students can use **Worksheet 1.4** to give their poems shape.

Plenary

- Ask some students to read their finished poems and ask the class for feedback. They should consider both strengths and weaknesses in their responses. Point to any particular techniques used and relate these to the work done in **Lessons 3** and **4**. Sum up by referring to the relevant text-type features in the Student Book, page 13.

Unit 1 Terror in the night

Worksheet 1.4: Writing a poem

1 Look up these words in a thesaurus to find some more that have the same meaning:

beat   cry   drip   sway   shadow   silence   quiver   rough

2 Now use some of the words above and think of others to write this poem. It has two verses. Give your poem a title when you have finished.

_____ (title)

At night when I hear the

tap

tap

tap

of the branch on the window,

And the _____

Above the _____

I feel _____ (repeating line)

At night when I _____

of the _____

And the _____

Below the _____

I feel _____

All in the mind

Terror in the night

Lesson

Framework Objectives

R7: Identify the main points, processes or ideas in a text and how they are sequenced and developed by the writer

Wr2: Collect, select and assemble ideas in a suitable planning format (flow chart)

Main text type: Argument

Student Book pages 19–24

Starter

- Explain to students that we can gain a quick impression of a text by looking at the first few words of each paragraph. **OHT 1.5**, in which students underline the first few words of each paragraph, can be used to demonstrate this.

Introduction

- Before reading the text, go through the glossary with the students. In particular, make sure that students understand the meaning of *alleged*, *environmental cues* and *clustered*. Explain that the last two are terms used by researchers.

Key Reading

- Read the website text to students, and then go through the key features of argument texts in the text-type box, emphasising the need to make points clearly and to refer to evidence supporting these points. Check understanding by asking these questions:
  - *What is evidence?*
  - *Why do we refer to evidence in an argument?*

Purpose

- Discuss the purpose of an argument text. Refer students to question **4** and ensure that they grasp that the purpose of this text is to demonstrate that ghosts do not exist.

Development

Reading for meaning

- Reiterate that in order to follow an argument we have to understand the topic of the argument, the main points being made and the evidence presented. Introduce the list of 'wh' questions on page 22, and go through the example questions, helping students to find where these are answered in the text (question **5**). Students should then draw up their own 'wh' questions (question **6a**) and ask a partner to answer these using evidence from the text.
- Remind students about the Starter activity. Then systematically go through the examples given on page 23, illustrating with the help of the flow chart how we can elicit the main points. Students can then complete the flow chart on their own or with a partner (question **7c**).

Plenary

- First sum up the strategies used to follow an argument and then ask students to sum up the argument in the text in their own words. Clarify any parts of the text which may not have been understood, and ensure that students are clear about the main points in preparation for the next lesson, which focuses on recording the evidence.

Unit 1 Terror in the night

OHT 1.5: Hacker horrors

1 Underline the first few words of each paragraph.

2 Use the underlined words to work out what each paragraph is about.

> Viruses are programs which are written deliberately to damage data. Viruses can hide themselves in a computer system. Some viruses are fairly harmless. Others have more serious effects. They can wipe out all your data or turn it into gobbledegook.
>
> A virus can infect your disks once it is in your computer. If you then lend them to someone or if your computer is part of a network, the virus will spread. The best way to combat a virus is with anti-virus software which makes computers safe from many types of virus.
>
> The Michelangelo virus was programmed to become active on March 6 1992, the 517th birthday of the Italian painter Michelangelo. It attacked computer systems throughout the world, turning data on hard disks into nonsense.
>
> When the Cascade virus attacks, all the letters in a file fall into a heap at the bottom of the screen. This looks spectacular but it's hard to see the funny side when it's your document.
>
> Criminals who get into computer systems without permission are called hackers. Using telephone lines, hackers link up their own computers to networks, so they can call up private files. By changing information in the files, they can steal money and goods without being caught.

From *Computers For Beginners* (Usborne)

Terror in the night

Framework Objective

S&L11: Adopt a range of roles in discussion and contribute in different ways
Main text type: Argument

Student Book page 24

Starter

- Write the terms *skimming* and *scanning* on the board. If students have met the terms before, ask them to describe the difference between the two skills and to give examples of when they would be useful, otherwise explain the terms and their usefulness to students.

Introduction

Focus on: Presenting the evidence

- Ensure students understand what the term *evidence* means. Refer back to the discussion on evidence in **Lesson 1** and ask students to:
  - *sum up its meaning*
  - *explain its importance in argument texts*
  - *explain the function of the evidence in this text* (i.e. to show that ghosts do not exist). Clarify any misunderstandings.
- In question **8**, ask students why it might be useful to scan the text for references to Dr Wiseman (i.e. because it will lead us to the evidence.) Discuss question **9**, noting that most evidence is found in the middle, after the description of the experiment. Help students locate the evidence and discuss it with them, after which they can complete question **10**.

Development

- Following question **10**, give students **Worksheet 1.6**, which they should complete on their own. Once completed correctly it will give a step-by-step account of the experiment and its outcomes. If necessary, go through this systematically with the class.

Key Speaking and Listening

- Students should work in groups to discuss whether ghosts exist. They need not make notes, but they should draw on the work they have done and put forward their own ideas. Encourage them to draw on expressions used in the student book (for example, *Scientists claim…*) and in **Worksheet 1.6** to help them articulate points. They should also share and challenge ideas. A spokesperson should be appointed to report back.

Plenary

- Once groups have reported back, discuss:
  - whether or not each group holds a unanimous point of view
  - whether any students changed their views through discussion.
- Ask students as a class to take a vote on whether or not they believe in ghosts.

Unit 1 Terror in the night

Worksheet 1.6: Step by step

Read all the starter sentences on the left first.
Then join each starter sentence with its correct half on the right by drawing a linking line.

Scientists carried out an experiment with…	… have these changes more than others.
The volunteers recorded unusual things…	…there are ghosts.
Results showed that certain places…	… such as changes in light and temperature.
When people feel these changes, they think…	…some volunteers in places supposed to be haunted.
So certain places become known…	…are all in the mind.
However, evidence suggests that ghosts…	…for being haunted.

Impact English Teacher's Resource © HarperCollinsPublishers 2005

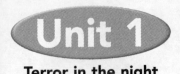

Terror in the night

Assessment Focus
AF1: Write imaginative, interesting and thoughtful texts
Main text type: Poetry

Student Book pages 25–27

You will need to have thesauruses available.

Starter
- The students will have common notions of what 'horror' is. These may be linked to horror films or macabre media images. Ask students to think of images of horror that have made an impression on them.

Introduction

Stage 1
- Encourage students to come up with their own simple images related to feelings of horror, beginning with the examples given in the Student Book. Remind them of the key features of poetry covered on page 13, particularly the work done on writing in lines and using repetition to create form.

Stage 2
- Go through the points outlined under Stage 2, helping students to create short evocative descriptions, which they should record and keep. Explain what similes and metaphors are, using the examples given. Students could create lines using either similes or metaphors. Others may be able to combine the two in one line. (See example on page 26.)

Development

Stage 3
- Students can now use the lines they have created to write a free-verse poem. They will progress at varying degrees, but they can be supported in their writing in the following ways:
  - Although the repeating structure of the lines will create form, also encourage students to try out different starting phrases (such as *I am*) until they settle on something they like.
  - Some students may be able to use non-finite verbs, for example, *skulking*. However, writing what they feel is more important than perfecting form. Encourage them to experiment.
  - Some students may find ending their poems difficult. Suggest that they read through their lines and listen to the rhythm to give them ideas. (For example, the rhythm could be broken in the last line by stopping abruptly: *The red-eyed monster…*) Once again, encourage students to try out various ideas.

Challenge
- Here students are asked to broaden the images they make by appealing to a range of senses. (Most of their original images will almost certainly appeal to sight.) An example of an image that appeals to the sense of touch is given for contrast. Ask students to create at least one line for each of the remaining senses and add the best to their poems.
Worksheet 1.7 can be used to help them compile a range of vocabulary.

Peer Assessment

- When students have completed their poems, they work in pairs and read each others' drafts. Write up the text-type features listed below and ask them to check if their drafts include them:
  - use of powerful images
  - use of regular or irregular rhythm
  - use of form-writing in lines, repeating words or phrases.
- They then fill in the Peer Assessment Sheet (see page 6) and feed back their findings.
- Students redraft according to suggestions.

Plenary

- Give a copy of **OHT 1.8** (top half only) to each group and get students to annotate the level 3 writing to show how well the student has incorporated the various features of poetry (images, rhythm and form) and what needs improvement. Then display the whole of **OHT 1.8** and ask for feedback on how to get the level 3 writing up to level 4. Show in the exemplar of level 4 how it can be done. Students can make changes to their own texts in light of this.
- Encourage students to read their poems aloud to the class. If appropriate, use their work to demonstrate further ways of creating variety in writing. For example:

  The red-eyed monster, lurking like a shadow

  could begin with the non-finite verb:

  Lurking like a shadow, the red-eyed monster...

Unit 1 — Terror in the night

Worksheet 1.7: The senses

The human senses are: **sight, sound, touch, taste, smell**.

1 What sense does each group of words below remind you of? Write down your answer.
   (Check words in a dictionary if you need to.)

sense:	
sour	acid
peppery	salty

sense:	
stench	musty
rancid	stinking

sense:	
twitching	smarting
gnaw	spasm

sense:	
clanging	muffled
booming	squawk

sense:	
squinting	crimson
blotch	dark

2 Add more words to each list. Make sure they remind you of the sense.

Unit 1 Terror in the night

OHT 1.8: Peer assessment

Assessment Focus

AF1: Write imaginative, interesting and thoughtful texts

Level 3

Horror is…
Like a red-eyed monster,
Like a sudden fever,
Like a cold sweat,
Like an icy chill,
Like the howl of a demon,
Like a ghost at midnight,
Rattling his bones.

Level 4

Horror is…
<u>Like</u> a red-eyed monster, ——— lines built around similes and verbs
<u>Waiting</u> for me,
Like a sudden fever,
Sweeping over me,
Like a cold sweat, ——— repetition gives form
Clinging to me,
Like an icy chill,
Piercing me,
Like a wild demon, ——— new verse introduced
Howling at me,

Like a ghost at midnight,
Clanging his chains ——— pattern changes to give a more interesting ending
<u>And rattling his bones</u>.

Impact English Teacher's Resource © HarperCollinsPublishers 2005

Unit 2
Myths and legends

Lesson 1

Framework Objective
R20: Explore the notion of literary heritage and understand why some texts have been particularly influential or significant
Main text type: Narrative

Student Book pages 28–31

Starter
- Brainstorm myths and fairy tales, writing several examples of each on the board. Then ask students to think about which are myths and which are fairy tales. Categorise each one by underlining it in a different colour. Divide the class into groups of 4 or 5 and ask them to come up with a definition of 'myth' and 'fairy tale'. Ask groups to feed back, and write class definitions on the board.

Introduction
- Read through the story together, checking that difficult words are understood.

Key Reading
- Run through the key features of narrative texts as shown in the text-type box. Check understanding by asking students these questions:
  - Think of another story that you are reading, or have just read. What is the main problem in the narrative?
  - Who are the main characters in that story?
  - 'It's a good book.' Say this in a different way that uses more powerful and interesting words.
- Students can complete question **1** on their own after discussion, or in pairs. Give them copies of **Worksheet 2.1** on which to draw their cartoon versions of the story; the first frame has been completed. Ask 3 or 4 pairs to show the class their answers, using the worksheet as an OHT, for others to comment. Conclude the section with class discussion of questions **2** and **3**.

Development
Purpose
- Students discuss questions **4** and **5** in pairs and feed back. For question **5**, you may want to brainstorm some difficult tasks that students have had to complete (from any stage in their life) in order to get their ideas flowing. During the feedback, ask if some of Heracles' qualities were shown in any way, for example, *bravery*, *strength* (including strength of mind), *persistence*, *cleverness*. This will prompt students to think about different qualities.

Plenary
- Ask students in groups to discuss why the story of Heracles has been told for hundreds of years. You may have to recap the story of Heracles' Twelve Labours. Discuss with them the structure of the story, asking them what the stages of the narrative are, to help them see what makes it a good narrative. Students then write down three things that make the story memorable or important. Feed back and discuss.

Unit 2 Myths and legends

Worksheet 2.1: Turning it into a cartoon

In pairs, discuss how you would turn the story into a cartoon. You have only four squares for your story. Write your ideas here:

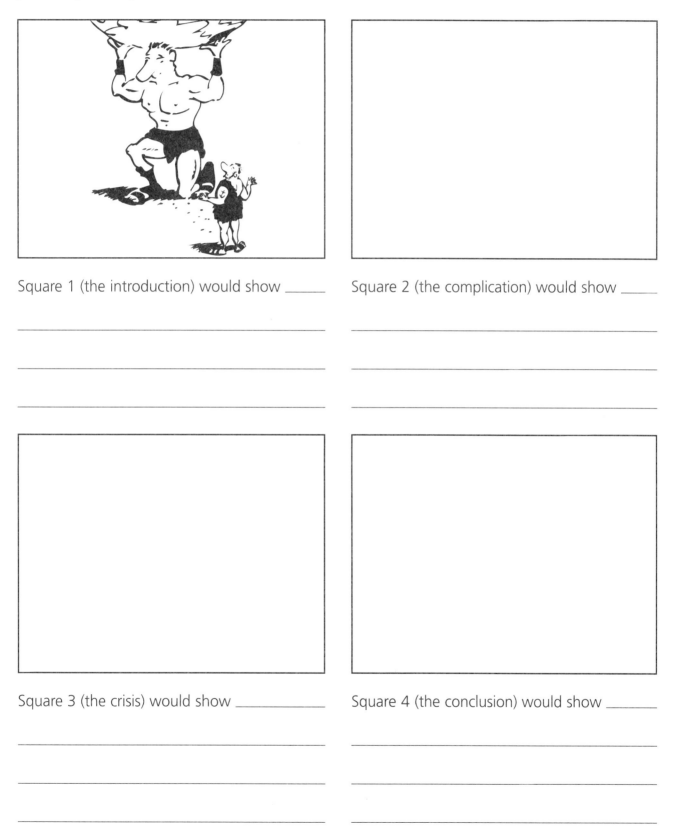

Square 1 (the introduction) would show _____
_____
_____

Square 2 (the complication) would show _____
_____
_____

Square 3 (the crisis) would show _____
_____
_____

Square 4 (the conclusion) would show _____
_____
_____

Impact English Teacher's Resource © HarperCollinsPublishers 2005

Myths and legends

Lesson

Framework Objectives

S18: Identify specific ways sentence structure and punctuation are different in older texts

R16: Distinguish between the attitudes and assumptions of the characters and those of the author

Main text type: Narrative

Student Book pages 32–34

Starter

- Write the following sentence on the board (from *Gulliver's Travels*, 1726), which is also about a giant, this time attacked by the tiny Lilliputians.

  But the creatures ran off a second time, before I could seize them; whereupon there was a great shout in a very shrill accent, and after it ceased, I heard one of them cry aloud, Tolgo phonac*; when in an instant I felt above an hundred arrows discharged on my left hand, which pricked me like so many needles; and besides, they shot another flight into the air, as we do bombs in Europe, whereof many, I suppose, fell on my body (though I felt them not), and some on my face, which I immediately covered with my left hand.*

- Read the sentence through with the class first, and make sure they understand it. In groups, they then discuss how the text differs from modern English. Ask them to consider:
  - sentence structure, for example, *length of sentence, phrases like 'I felt them not'*
  - punctuation, for example, *semicolons, number of commas (marking pauses)*
  - word choice, for example, *words that are not often used today.*
- Ask 2 or 3 groups to feed back, with examples.

Introduction

Reading for meaning

- Ask students to answers question **6** orally, then read through the section together, emphasising the three main ways of building up a character and how the examples show this. Students answer question **7** in pairs or on their own, and feed back. Students attempt question **8** in pairs. For reinforcement, or as an alternative, give pairs a set of cards (**Worksheet 2.2**) to match up. There are three examples (in italics) of what Atlas says, three examples of what Atlas does, and two examples of what Atlas looks like. Each example has an 'effect' card which shows how the description builds up a picture of the character. Students must match each example with an effect card, and group them in the three main categories. Ask 3 or 4 pairs to present their results and ask the class to comment.

Development

Focus on: Sentence structure

- Read this section with the class, bringing out the effect of the shorter sentences in the reading. Ensure they understand what a clause is. Refer back to text in the Starter to make an effective comparison between sentence length in the two texts. You may also like to ask students to look at the next few lines in the story (lines 26–33) and to discuss what effect the sentence length has there.

Key Writing

- Students complete questions **10** and **11** on their own. Work with a group of weaker students on question **11**, discussing ideas for story development (*how Atlas approached the dragon, the dragon's reaction, etc.*) and focusing on sentence structure and building up character.

Plenary

- Ask 3 or 4 students to read out their paragraphs. The rest of the class should comment on:
  - the effectiveness of the sentence structure
  - how well the writer builds up the character(s).

Unit 2 Myths and legends

Worksheet 2.2: Building up a character

What Atlas does

He has the task of 'holding up the sky and keeping the stars from falling'

This shows how incredibly strong he must be

He 'stretched himself, then strode away towards the end of the world'

This shows how sore Atlas must have been, and what giant steps he took

He 'took charge of the sky again'

This shows that Atlas has been taken in by Heracles' trick

What Atlas says

"How can I go anywhere?"

This shows how puzzled and annoyed Atlas must be

"Could you? Would you? Then I'll do it!"

This shows how delighted Atlas is at the thought of handing the sky over to Heracles

"I'm going to let you go on holding up the sky, and I'll deliver these apples."

This shows how determined Atlas is to be free

What Atlas looks like

'Now Atlas was no ordinary giant, as big as a house'

This shows that he was much bigger than a house

'The sun scorched his neck and the new moon shaved his beard'

This shows how tall Atlas was – he reached the stars

Unit 2
Myths and legends
Lesson 3

Framework Objective
W14: Define and deploy words with precision, including their exact implication in context
Main text type: Explanation

Student Book pages 35–38

Starter

- Brainstorm words beginning with 'super'. Write them on the board, and suggest examples if necessary (*supervise, superintendent, superb*). Ask students to underline different word classes in different colours. Determine what the prefix 'super' means from seeing what all the words have in common ('super' is Latin for 'above', 'over', 'higher'). If students haven't already mentioned 'superman', ask them what the word means.

Introduction

- Read the website text aloud to the class, checking that difficult words are understood.

Key Reading

- Go through the key features of explanation texts as shown in the text-type box. Check understanding by asking students these questions:
  – *What does 'logical' mean? Why is it important for explanation texts to be logical?*
  – *In the sentence 'If danger threatens, Clark Kent turns into Superman', which bit is the cause and which the effect?*
  – *What is a glossary?*
- Students discuss questions **1** to **3** in pairs. Then ask 2 or 3 pairs to feed back their answers for the class to comment on.

Development

Purpose

- Ask students to look at question **4** on their own, then ask individuals for their answers (and reasons). Encourage students to word their answers in causal language (for example: *I think the purpose of this text is to explain why Superman is so powerful. This is because…*).

Reading for meaning

- Emphasise the importance of a clear and logical order to the steps in explanation texts. Then give out the cards on **Worksheet 2.3** to pairs of students; their task in question **5** is to arrange the cards into a logical order that shows the steps in the explanation. They will need to refer to the text to help them. Present the cards on an OHT, asking pairs to present one step at a time. You may wish to explain that what they are creating is a flow chart. Students then attempt question **6** on their own.

Plenary

- Students write down three key features of explanation texts, without referring to their textbooks.

Unit 2 Myths and legends

Worksheet 2.3: Ordering an explanation

E Superman comes from Krypton. But he can survive on Earth.	
	**G** So Krypton would have weighed 1321 times as much as Earth.
C So Krypton must have had the same climate and atmosphere as Earth.	
	**D** So the gravity of Krypton was at least ten times as strong as Earth's.
A So Krypton was probably made of rocks and water, and had a metal core, like Earth.	
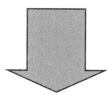	**B** So lifting an object would take Superman ten times less effort than on Krypton.
F Krypton was the size of Jupiter. Jupiter is 1321 times the size of Earth.	

Impact English Teacher's Resource © HarperCollinsPublishers 2005

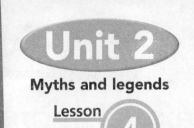

Unit 2
Myths and legends
Lesson 4

Framework Objectives

Wr12: Explain a process logically, highlighting the links between cause and effect

S&L14: Acknowledge other people's views, justifying or modifying their own views in the light of what others say

Main text type: Explanation

Student Book pages 39–40

Starter

- Brainstorm different kinds of explanation texts, and write them on the board. Then choose two or three of them, and ask for made-up examples of causal language from them. For example:
  - *When you press lever F, the pebble falls into the hole.*
  - *Recounts are usually written in the past tense because they relate what has happened in the past.*

  Write these on the board in the form of full sentences, and show the students what makes the language causal in each case.

Introduction

Focus on: Highlighting cause and effect

- Read through the section, which should reinforce what has been learned in the Starter. Ensure that students understand the meaning and purpose of causal connectives. Look back at the examples in the Starter, if necessary, and identify the connectives. Can they add any to the list in their book?
- Students then attempt questions **7** and **8** in pairs. Tell them that their examples may consist of a single sentence, unlike the example in their book, as it may be two clauses that are linked in a causal way, rather than two sentences. Ask pairs to present their answers to the class, on the board or OHT.
- To reinforce students' understanding, give out copies of **Worksheet 2.4** for students to work on in pairs. This provides an alternative explanation text which students analyse by highlighting the causal language, and in particular the connectives.

Development

Key Writing

- Read through the section with the class to ensure they understand what the task is. Students work in pairs. They should talk through their explanation with a partner and listen to their comments on these questions:
  - *Is their explanation organised in a clear and logical way?*
  - *Does it use connectives to highlight cause and effect?*
- They then alter their explanation in the light of their partner's comments, before writing it down. Ensure that the partners listen out for causal language, and that this is then used in the written version. Try to discourage students from simply copying the text in the bullet points. The final stage is a proofcheck, which includes checking the appropriateness of the language for the given audience.

Plenary

- Ask 3 or 4 students to read out their explanations, or present them on an OHT to the class. Invite class comment on:
  - how effective the explanations are (above all, the use of causal language)
  - how suitable the texts are for the audience in mind (seven-year-olds).

Unit 2 Myths and legends

Worksheet 2.4: Causal language

1 Highlight all the examples of causal language in this passage. Underline the causal connectives.

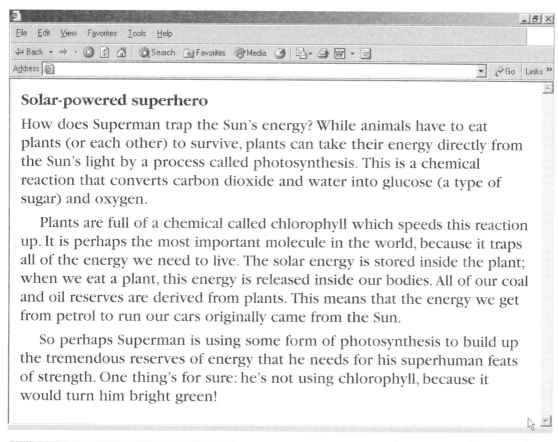

Solar-powered superhero

How does Superman trap the Sun's energy? While animals have to eat plants (or each other) to survive, plants can take their energy directly from the Sun's light by a process called photosynthesis. This is a chemical reaction that converts carbon dioxide and water into glucose (a type of sugar) and oxygen.

Plants are full of a chemical called chlorophyll which speeds this reaction up. It is perhaps the most important molecule in the world, because it traps all of the energy we need to live. The solar energy is stored inside the plant; when we eat a plant, this energy is released inside our bodies. All of our coal and oil reserves are derived from plants. This means that the energy we get from petrol to run our cars originally came from the Sun.

So perhaps Superman is using some form of photosynthesis to build up the tremendous reserves of energy that he needs for his superhuman feats of strength. One thing's for sure: he's not using chlorophyll, because it would turn him bright green!

From www.bbc.co.uk/sn

solar from the Sun
molecule a very small particle

2 Write the causal connectives in this box. Add any others that you found on the Superman website in your Student Book (pages 35–36).

Written in the stars?

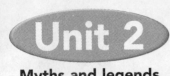

Myths and legends

Lesson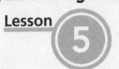

Framework Objectives

S8: Recognise the cues to start a new paragraph and use the first sentence to orientate the reader

S13f: Revise the stylistic conventions of discursive writing

Main text type: Discursive

Student Book pages 41–46

Starter

- Brainstorm words ending with 'logy' or 'ology'. Write them on the board, suggesting examples if necessary. After students identify what all the words have in common, determine that the suffix 'ology' means 'the science of (or study of)' and explain where it comes from ('logos' is Greek for 'word'). If students haven't already mentioned 'astrology', ask them what the word means ('astro' is Greek for 'star').

Introduction

- Read the article aloud to the class, checking that difficult words are understood.

Key Reading

- Go through the key features of discursive texts as shown in the text-type box. Check understanding by asking students these questions:
  - *Where are discursive texts likely to be found?*
  - *Give some different phrases that indicate point of view.*
  - *What is formal language? Give some examples.*
- Students discuss questions **1** to **3** in pairs. Then ask 2 or 3 pairs to feed back their answers for the class to comment on.

Development

Purpose

- Discuss what the purpose of a discursive text is. Refer students to question **4** and ask them to consider their answer in pairs. Note that answers **a** and **b** can both be argued for – only **c** is actually wrong.

Reading for meaning

- Students think about questions **5** to **7** individually, and answer them orally.
- Read the section 'Using paragraphs' with the class and ensure they understand what a paragraph is (and how to make one), before discussing the idea of topic sentences (although this term is not actually used). Students then work in pairs on question **8**, using the paragraph analysed in their book as a model. Ask 2 or 3 pairs to present their answers on an OHT.
- Students who need more help with identifying paragraphs and topic sentences can be given **Worksheet 2.5**, which provides an additional discursive text for paragraph analysis.

Plenary

- Ask students to write down three key features of discursive texts, without referring to their textbooks.

Impact English Teacher's Resource © HarperCollins*Publishers* 2005

Unit 2 Myths and legends

Worksheet 2.5: Paragraphs

Top scientist backs astrology

Star movements 'can influence us'

1   A university lecturer in astronomy, Dr Percy Seymour, has shocked the scientific world by publishing a book called *The Scientific Proof of Astrology*. In it he suggests that human brain development is affected by the Earth's magnetic field, especially when the baby is in the womb. And – this is the key point - the Earth's magnetic field is interfered with by the movement of the planets.

2   Seymour's theory has met with a barrage of criticism from other scientists. 'It's right up there with stuff like crop circles being made by extra-terrestrials,' says Robert Massey, astronomer at the Royal Observatory.

3   Most scientists dismiss his arguments because the changes in the Earth's magnetic field, which are supposed to account for our behaviour, are so tiny. According to one leading astronomer, you get a far stronger magnetic field from your lights and washing machine!

4   Astrologers, however, were delighted with Professor Seymour's claims. They are especially pleased that a former scientist has come out in their favour. Russell Grant, the astrologer, said, 'At last someone is not just saying, "It's a load of poppycock."'

5   Many in public life would agree, though they might keep it quiet. The former American president, Ronald Reagan, admitted that he consulted astrologers before making important decisions. Even the take-off times for Air Force One relied on the movement of the planets.

1 a What is the purpose of the first paragraph in this news article?

  b Which sentence makes it clear what this paragraph is about?

2 The second paragraph has only two sentences. The sentences had to be written in this order. Why?

3 a Which paragraph describes how astrologers have reacted to Professor Seymour's book?

  b Why did the writer start a new paragraph at this point?

4 Which sentence makes it clear what the last paragraph is about?

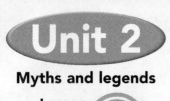

Unit 2
Myths and legends
Lesson 6

Framework Objectives

R9: Distinguish between the views of the writer and those expressed by others in the text
S&L10: Identify and report the main points emerging from discussion
Main text type: Discursive

Student Book pages 46–47

Starter

- Write the first three sentences of the article on the board (lines 1–3). In groups of 4, students identify and write down the words that include a long 'ee' sound ('leap', 'week', 'magazines', 'we', 'being'), then supply as many others with the same spellings as they can (total time for activity is five minutes).

Introduction

Focus on: Presenting different views

- Read through this section with the class. Ensure that students understand the difference between direct and reported speech. Give several other examples on the board, especially ones with a reporting verb in the past tense (which result in different tenses being used for the reported speech).
- Students then attempt question **9** in pairs. You may need to list several reporting verbs on the board, including 'find that', to give a clue. Ask 3 or 4 pairs to present their answers on an OHT for the class to comment on.
- **Worksheet 2.6** offers further work on direct and reported speech. In the first question, students will need to:
  – choose an introductory phrase
  – change tenses
  – use pronouns where necessary.

Development

Key Speaking and Listening

- Read through the section with the class. Students should not write down their own views (or those of others), but work orally and keep others' views in mind. The work done on **Worksheet 2.6** may help as preparation, however. Ensure students understand that summarising the discussion can be a mixture of reported speech and direct speech.

Plenary

- Ask 3 or 4 students to present their summaries. Invite class comment on:
  – how effective they are as oral discursive texts
  – how varied the summaries are in terms of reporting clauses and direct/reported mix.

Unit 2 Myths and legends

Worksheet 2.6: Direct/reported speech

Here is Greg's view about astrology. It is written using direct speech.

> "I'm a typical Aries – independent and active. It all makes sense to me," said Greg.

If you now **report** Greg's speech, this summary is from your own point of view. That is why pronouns and tenses are changed (the underlined words):

> Greg said that <u>he was</u> a typical Aries – independent and active. It all <u>made</u> sense to <u>him</u>.

Note also that speech marks are not used. This is because Greg's exact words have not been quoted.

- "Science doesn't have all the answers!" – Chenise
- "Star signs just pigeonhole people. We're all different, after all." – Kimberly

1 Now choose one of the views above. Discuss with a partner how you would turn the **direct** speech into **reported** speech. Then write it down below. Underline the words that have been changed.

_____

_____

2 Write down your partner's views on astrology (a) quoted **directly**, and (b) **reported**.

a _____

b _____

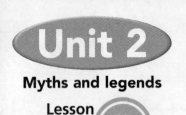

Myths and legends

Lesson 7

Assessment Focuses

AF2: Produce texts which are appropriate to task, reader and purpose
AF4: Construct paragraphs and use cohesion within and between paragraphs
Main text type: Discursive

Student Book pages 48–49

Starter

- Ask students to jot down three main features of discursive texts, then to feed back to the class. Present the task to the students as outlined in their book, and ask them how the main features just explored relate to the specific task of writing a review of reviews. For example, if they have said 'presenting a series of points on both sides', ask them what the different sides will be in this case.

Introduction

Stage 1

- Read through Stage 1 with the class. In small groups, students then work out how to organise the notes so that they form the basis of three paragraphs of text. Ask one or two groups to feed back to the class, so that everyone is on the right lines.

Development

Stage 2

- In this stage, students should work in the same groups to draft their piece. Go through the composing reminders and refer students to the relevant sections of the chapter for further detail.
- Work with 1 or 2 low-ability groups to share progress, deal with questions and problems, and celebrate achievement. At the end of this stage, share good examples of student writing with the class, but also ask how the drafts presented could be improved. Model one or two examples on the board. Give students copies of **Worksheet 2.7** to help them draft their writing.

Peer Assessment

- When students have completed their writing, they work in pairs and read each others' drafts. Write up the text-type features listed below and ask them to check if their drafts include them.
    - form consists of opening statement, points on both sides of the issue and a conclusion
    - use of phrases at start of sentences signalling which side of the issue is going to be covered
    - use of formal language.
- Students fill in their Peer Assessment Sheet (see page 6) and feed back their findings.
- Students redraft according to suggestions.

Impact English Teacher's Resource © HarperCollinsPublishers 2005

Plenary

- Give a copy of **OHT 2.8** (top half only) to each group and get students to annotate the level 3 writing to show how well the student has used paragraphs and produced a text appropriate to its purpose and what needs improvement. Then display the whole of **OHT 2.8** and ask for feedback on how to get the level 3 writing up to level 4. Show in the exemplar of level 4 how it can be done. Students make changes to their own texts in light of this.
- Ask 2 or 3 students to read out or present their reviews. The class can then give constructive criticism of how well they show the features of discursive writing.

Unit 2 Myths and legends

Worksheet 2.7: Writing your review

Use the grid below to write notes on your review of reviews.

Title:
1st paragraph   Write notes on the introduction here. Give some background to the film.   _____   _____   Jot down your opening sentence, e.g. 'The papers are full of news and views about *Troy*.'   _____   _____
2nd paragraph   Write notes on what *The Morning News* says here.   _____   _____   Jot down some phrases to signal the point of view, e.g. 'According to *The Morning News* …'   _____   _____
3rd paragraph   Write notes on what *The Evening Star* says here.   _____   _____   Jot down some phrases to signal the point of view, e.g. '*The Evening Star*, however, …'   _____   _____

Unit 2 — Myths and legends

OHT 2.8: Peer assessment

Assessment Focuses
AF2: Produce texts which are appropriate to task, reader and purpose
AF4: Construct paragraphs and use cohesion within and between paragraphs

Level 3

'The Morning News' said there was 'wooden acting'. 'The Evening Star' really liked the film. 'The Morning News' said 'Give me 'Gladiator' any day'. The other paper said it is 'The movie of the year' so it must have liked it. The paper described the star – Brad Pitt – as a 'sulky, beefy hunk'.

Level 4

> 'The Morning News' also thought that the acting was wooden. It liked 'Gladiator' better.
>
> The paper called 'The Evening Star' really liked the film. It said it is the movie of the year so it must have liked it. 'The Evening Star' described the star – Brad Pitt – as a 'sulky, beefy hunk'. 'Troy' cost 200 million to make.

Annotations:
- new paragraph started here, as we are now reading about *The Evening Star's* views
- now an effective mixture of direct quotes and summaries of what the papers said
- this paragraph is now all about what *The Morning News* thought
- good phrase at start of sentence signalling the point of view being described
- this sentence gives evidence for the sentence before

Alien visitors

Out of this world

Lesson 1

Framework Objectives

R8: Infer and deduce meanings using evidence in the text, identifying where and how meanings are implied
S13f: Revise the stylistic conventions of discursive writing
Main text type: Discursive

Student Book pages 50–53

Starter

- Write these two sentences up on the board:
  - *Conditions on the planet Mars are not suitable to support life forms.*
  - *It seems unlikely that conditions on the planet Mars can support life forms.*
- Use these sentences to explain the difference between explicit meanings and implied meanings. The first leaves the reader in no doubt that there is no life on Mars by stating this explicitly. In contrast, the second leaves the possibility open by allowing the reader to infer through the verb 'seems' and 'can' and the adverb 'unlikely' the implied meaning that there may be life on Mars. Ask students to come up with other versions of the sentence that will allow a reader to infer implicit or hidden meanings. Use **Worksheet 3.1** to allow students to explore these ideas.

Introduction

- Read the website text through with the class, making sure any difficult words in the glossary are understood. Then elicit from 1 or 2 students what the text is about.

Key Reading

- Go through the key features of discursive texts as shown in the text-type box. Check understanding by asking students these questions:
  - *Which two views are put forward?*
  - *What kinds of evidence are included?*
- Then get students to discuss questions **1** to **3** in pairs. Help less able students with question **1** by prompting them to think why the past tense is suitable for the type of information in paragraph 4. Invite 2 or 3 pairs to feed back their answers and ask the class to comment.

Development

Purpose

- In question **4**, pairs discuss the options given for the main purpose of the website text and decide which is its main purpose. Encourage them to explore whether there are elements of the other purposes also present in the text.
- Introduce the terms 'fact' and 'opinion' and refer back to the work done on explicit meanings (linked to facts) and implied meanings (more often linked to opinions) in the Starter. Pairs then reread the extract to identify facts and opinions in question **5**. Before they tackle **5c**, point out that in balanced discursive writing the writer's opinions are not usually made clear and then ask them if they can detect the writer's opinion in this case. They should support their answers with at least one piece of evidence from the text.
- To extend the work, give each pair a copy of **Worksheet 3.1** and ask them to identify which are facts and which are opinions about alien life.

Plenary

- Recap with students the three main features of discursive writing without reference to the book. Elicit from them why it is important to be able to distinguish between facts and opinions in a discursive text.

Unit 3 Out of this world

Worksheet 3.1: Fact or opinion

Below are some statements about life on other planets. Place an 'F' next to the statement if it is a Fact and an 'O' next to the statement if it is an Opinion.

We have received no communication from other intelligent life forms.	
It is not very likely that Earth is the only planet with life on it.	
Billions of stars have planets around them.	
Many people think that aliens exist.	
Superior alien life forms would be hostile.	
Communication with aliens would be difficult.	
The distances between stars are too great for communication.	
Crop circles prove that aliens have landed.	
Many people have been abducted by aliens.	
Things like crop circles are difficult to explain.	

Unit 3
Out of this world

Framework Objectives

R8: Infer and deduce meanings using evidence in the text, identifying where and how meanings are implied

Wr10: Organise texts in ways appropriate to their content and signpost this clearly to the reader

S&L12: Use exploratory, hypothetical and speculative talk as a way of researching ideas and expanding thinking

Main text type: Discursive

Student Book pages 53–55

Starter

- Ask students to recap on the two main points of view expressed in the website text. Then explain that the structure of the text and the way these views are signalled for the reader will be the main focus of this lesson.

Reading for meaning

- Ask pairs to scan the text again for the answers to questions **6** to **9**. Ensure that students understand that essentially they are looking for two pieces of evidence that support each view. Invite 1 or 2 pairs to feed back with their answers.
- Question **10** asks how the questions in the conclusion help the reader weigh up the two views presented. Ask the class how effective this is.

Introduction

Focus on: Assessing the content of discursive texts

- If students are struggling in question **11** to extract the two balancing points for each view from paragraphs 2 to 5, **Worksheet 3.2** (which provides these points as cut out cards) may be of help. It also includes some evidence cards which students can be asked to place with the points they support for question **12**.
- Return to the role of linking phrases in discursive texts which signpost which view is coming next, before students tackle question **13**. Encourage them to experiment with different verbs to reflect on the difference this makes to the strength of the view being put forward.

Development

Key Writing

- Pairs begin their work on question **14** by discussing the bullet points provided and adding any more they can think of, based on the website text or their own experiences, for example, some might refer to many of the ideas about space and alien life in *Star Trek* are based on scientific facts/theories. The emphasis here should be on exploring a range of points before they settle on their main points.
- Students then progress to writing their own discursive text, remembering to introduce their topic, give a series of balanced points, and then conclude by asking what the reader thinks. Remind them to signpost the different views expressed, using some of the bulleted suggestions.

Plenary

- Ask 1 or 2 students to read out their discursive text and invite the class to comment on how balanced each piece is and how clear the points are to follow. The class should also try to gauge how many points are factual and how many give opinions.

Unit 3 Out of this world

Worksheet 3.2: Points for and against

View 1 – Points for

View 2 – Points against

First documented sightings 1850s	Explained by natural phenomena
Biblical references to fiery objects in sky	Explained by ball lightning
Ancient man genetically altered by aliens	Most UFOs turn out to be identifiable after all
Cylindrical or cigar shaped objects in the sky	

Evidence cards

Evidence: 1940s UFO sightings hit the headlines	**Evidence:** Explanation for 'missing link' in human evolution
Evidence: High range weather balloons mistaken for UFOs	

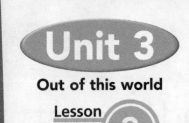

Unit 3
Out of this world
Lesson 3

Framework Objectives

S3: Use punctuation to clarify meaning, particularly at the boundaries between sentences and clauses

R8: Infer and deduce meanings using evidence in the text, identifying where and how meanings are implied

Main text type: Narrative

Student Book pages 56–60

Starter

- Explain to the class that they are about to read a passage with some unusual punctuation which ignores some rules about punctuating sentences and parts of sentences. Ask students for some general punctuation rules (for example, *sentences start with capital letters and end with a full stop; don't run sentences together linking them with commas; use a comma between a subordinate clause and a main clause; use pairs of commas around a relative clause to separate it off*) and write these on the board or an OHT. Consolidate work on conventional boundary punctuation with **Worksheet 3.3**.

Introduction

- Inform students that they are about to read a passage of fiction which features aliens. Ask them to recall some of the fictional aliens they have encountered in novels, films, TV and computer games and to express some of their views on the likely behaviour of aliens. Read the extract from *Only You Can Save Mankind*, making sure any difficult glossary words are understood.

Key Reading

- Go through the key features of narrative texts as shown in the text-type box. Check understanding by asking students these questions:
  – Exactly where does the 'problem' arise in the extract?
  – Who is the narrator of the story?
  – What would be the effect on the paragraph if 'Stars roared past...' was cut from line 17?
- Get students to discuss questions **1** to **3** in pairs. Refer to the summary of the usual punctuation/layout for direct speech in **Unit 9** (page 197 of the Student Book) as a reminder before students tackle question **3**. Invite 2 or 3 pairs to feed back their answers and ask the class to comment.

Development

Purpose

- This section focuses particularly on how the extract, as a novel opening, draws the reader in. Encourage pairs to discuss each of the features mentioned in question **4**. Question **5** explores the slight ambiguity of the opening, which also keeps the reader guessing for the first fifteen lines.

Reading for meaning

- The initial focus in this section is on close reading of the extract. Questions **6** to **9** test out students' ability to extract information and infer meaning from the opening.
- The focus shifts with question **10** to the paragraph structure of the opening. Elicit through students' answers that the short paragraphs help reflect the pace of the action and Johnny's excitement. The single-word paragraph 'Ah!' (line 28) signals a pause in the game.

Plenary

- Ask students to reflect on their comments about the likely behaviour of the aliens and compare them to the behaviour of the aliens in the opening – how has the writer both met and challenged their expectations? Elicit from students three features of narrative texts that this extract displays.

Unit 3 Out of this world

Worksheet 3.3: Sentence boundaries

Punctuation can show a break or a pause in a text, but also helps the reader to understand the meaning of a sentence

1 Punctuate the following sentences correctly.

  a The postman who comes from Manchester comes to our school twice a day

  b If you think it's a good idea you could sleep on in the morning

  c As I was sitting on a wall reading my book the bus came to take me to school

  d The train came into the station I was pleased to get on

2 The following sentences are incorrectly punctuated. Put a ring round the mistakes.

  a We had ham beans and salad for lunch: it wasn't very filling.

  b Many people claim to have been abducted by aliens: however few people believe them.

  c It used to be said that the Great Wall of China; the largest man made object on earth; was visible from the moon, this is not true.

Framework Objectives

R15: Trace the ways in which a writer structures a text to prepare a reader for the ending, and comment on the effectiveness of the ending

Wr6: Portray character, directly and indirectly, through description, dialogue and action

S&L12: Use exploratory, hypothetical and speculative talk as a way of researching ideas and expanding thinking

Main text type: Narrative

Student Book pages 60–62

Starter

- Ask students to share their knowledge of computer game types. These might include: *shoot 'em up, simulations, real time adventure, net-based games, puzzles*, and so on. Make a list of the game types on the board. Get them to explore the language that has been coined for these game types. Ask students to identify the type of game being played by Johnny in *Only You Can Save Mankind* (i.e. a shoot 'em up game).

Introduction

- Remind students of the extract from the previous lesson and explain that you will be considering how successful it is as a story opening and speculating how the story ends.

Focus on: Successful story openings

- Run through the bulleted features of a compelling story opening. Then ask students to reread the extract, analysing which of these techniques is used effectively for question **11**. Invite 2 or 3 students to feed back to the class.
- Pairs follow this up by completing question **12** which highlights other features of the opening that engage the reader. Pairs then report back to the class on their findings.

Development

- The focus now moves to the possible ending of the story. Use the bullets in question **13** to prompt students to speculate on how the story develops. They should find evidence in the extract for the option they choose.
- To extend this work further, provide each student with a copy of **Worksheet 3.4**, which is the end of the novel. This will allow students to discuss how well the story is set up by the opening and how well the ending works. They will also be able to reflect on the predictions they made in question **13**.
- Students might also like to discuss the implication of the final screen shot. What would happen if Johnny pressed 'Y'? Would the ending have been better without it?

Key Writing

- Students draw on their analysis of a story opening to write their own in question **14**. Encourage them to plan their story fully, using the headings provided by the grid in the Student Book. Guide a group in brainstorming exciting opening events and potential 'problems'. Share the best ideas and encourage pairs to comment constructively on how the plans can be improved. Guide the drafting, praising any particularly successful sentences.

Plenary

- Ask 1 or 2 students to present their story plans and then read their openings. Invite class comment on how well the writing used the plan. Encourage them also to speculate on how each story might end.

Unit 3 Out of this world

Worksheet 3.4: A good ending?

Below is the ending of *Only You Can Save Mankind*.

> He snuggled down, treasuring this time stolen between dreaming and waking.
>
> So… what next? He'd have to talk to Kirsty, who dreamed of being Sigourney and forgot that she was trying to be someone who was *acting*. And he had a suspicion that he'd see his parents before long.
>
> He was probably going to be talked at a lot, but at least that'd make a change.
>
> These were still Trying Times. There was still school. Nothing actually was better, probably. No one was doing anything with a magic wand.
>
> But the fleet had got away. Compared to that, everything else was… well, not easy. But less like a wall and more like steps.
>
> You might never win, but at least you could try. If not you, who else?
>
> He turned over and went back to sleep.
>
> The Border hung in the sky.
>
> Huge white letters, thousands of miles high. They spelled:
>
>
>
> And the fleet roared past. Tankers, battleships, fighters… they soared and rolled, their shadows streaking across the letters as ship after ship escaped, for ever.
>
>

From *Only You Can Save Mankind*
by Terry Pratchett

With a partner discuss:

1 Do you think this is a good ending to the story?

2 Did you guess that the book might end like this? What clues did the opening give you?

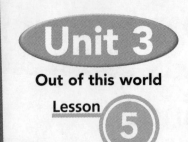

Unit 3
Out of this world
Lesson 5

Framework Objectives

R8: Infer and deduce meanings using evidence in the text, identifying where and how meanings are implied

S&L12: Use exploratory, hypothetical and speculative talk as a way of researching ideas and expanding thinking

Main text type: Explanation

Student Book pages 63–66

Starter

- Brainstorm with the class all the different subjects and situations in which they give or are given explanations. Write these up on the board. Emphasise that these can be written or spoken explanations (for example, *a written explanation of a scientific process, explaining where you have been to your parents*).
- This discussion will enable you to tease out the difference between information and explanation, i.e. that information tells the reader *what* something is like; explanation tells the reader *why* or *how* something is as it is. It may also clear up any confusion between instruction and explanation. Highlight the fact that understanding how explanations work is a key to grasping new ideas in many different subjects.

Introduction

- Explain to students that this lesson is to be about how real aliens might have adapted to environmental conditions on their home planet. Ask students to give examples of how animals on earth are adapted to their environment, for example, *giraffes* or *dolphins*. Read the *Alien Life* extract, making sure any difficult glossary words are understood.

Key Reading

- Go through the key features of explanation texts as shown in the table. Check understanding by asking students these questions:
  - *Why is it important for explanation texts to be logical?*
  - *How does causal language help make an explanation clear?*
  - *Why are technical terms necessary to many explanations?*
- Then get students to discuss questions **1** to **3** in pairs. Before they complete question **2**, read the explanation of 'connective' in the 'Grammar for reading' panel and give some examples in context. Invite 2 or 3 pairs to feed back their answers and ask the class to comment.

Development

Purpose

- Students begin to analyse in question **4** how the text uses examples to help explain its main points. **Worksheet 3.5** provides all the main points and examples as cut out cards. Hand out a set of cards to each pair. Get them first to reread the text and identify the main points. Then they group each one with its examples. Consolidate the work done by using an OHT of the complete worksheet.

Reading for meaning

- The focus in this section is on close reading of the extract. Questions **5** to **8** test out students' ability to locate specific points in the explanation text. This may lead to further discussion of the technical terms around which the questions are based.

Plenary

- Ask students to reflect on how this explanation might have been different if aimed at a much younger audience. What would need to change in the text? Recap on the main features of explanation texts to help them consider this.

Unit 3 Out of this world

Worksheet 3.5: Using examples

Life on Earth developed through evolution	Feathers, leaves, flowers, legs, feet and eyes evolved in particular conditions on Earth
So unlikely that on other planets there will be donkeys and slugs	Different planets have different conditions
Aliens could be 'little and green', but unlikely to be 'men'	Life on other planets will be different
Life on Earth depends on a mix of nitrogen, oxygen and carbon dioxide	Different atmospheres would create completely different life forms
How life on other planets might fit into the environments there	A large planet with strong gravity might have small creatures
A planet with an atmosphere containing sulphuric acid might have creatures with strong outer coatings	Planets made up of gases might have creatures that are buoyant or have wings

Unit 3
Out of this world
Lesson 6

Framework Objectives

Wr10: Organise texts in ways appropriate to their content and signpost this clearly to the reader

S&L6: Listen for and recall the main points of a talk, reading or television programme, reflecting on what has been heard to ask searching questions, make comments or challenge the views expressed

S&L12: Use exploratory, hypothetical and speculative talk as a way of researching ideas and expanding thinking

Main text type: Explanation

Student Book pages 66–67

Starter

- Elicit from students how they talk about future events. Write up any phrases they come up with that include the future tense of modal verbs. Use these to distinguish between the future tense and the language of possibility in all its forms (for example, *might*, *could*, *may*, as well as phrases like, *it's possible that*). Introduce the term 'modal verbs' only if they are ready for it.

Introduction

Focus on: The structure of an explanation text

- The initial focus of this section in question **9** is again the structure of the text, but this time students are asked to look at whether the explanation could be ordered differently and how. Hand out an intact version of **Worksheet 3.5** to groups, which students will be familiar with. This will remind them of the current structure and can be cut up by students to explore different orderings of the main points. Groups then feed back with their ideas to the class.
- In question **10**, students look closely at the use of phrases that indicate possibility in the text. Explain that although this is not a usual feature of scientific writing, it is appropriate in a text speculating on whether or not something exists. Students can draw on the examples on the board from the Starter.
- To extend this work on modal verbs and the language of possibility, students can explore degrees of uncertainty and possibility through **Worksheet 3.6**.

Development

Key Writing

- In responding to question **12**, students should be encouraged to think imaginatively about their chosen topic. The bullets provided should help them come up with the content and examples they will need to complete in detail. However, they also need to be reminded to use the language of explanation, to make each point clearly, showing the cause and effect or the *why* of each main point. Also encourage them to express themselves in terms of possibility rather than the certainty implied by the simple present or a future tense. Model this opening sentence to show these ideas…

    My ideal room <u>would</u> have red walls, <u>because</u> I love loud colours and red <u>would</u> make me feel warm all the time.

Plenary

- Invite 2 or 3 students to share their explanations. Ask the rest of the class, when listening to these, to pay particular attention to words expressing cause and possibility or degrees of certainty.

Unit 3 Out of this world

Worksheet 3.6: Possibilities

We often use words like *might*, *could* and *should* when we refer to the future or to things we are uncertain about.

1 Read the sentences below and then pick the description that best matches the meaning from the choices given.

a I **might** go to the cinema tomorrow.
  i. Will definitely go
  ii. Would like to go
  iii. Am thinking about going
  iv. Have permission to go

b I **could** go to the cinema tomorrow.
  i. Would like to go
  ii. Am thinking about going
  iii. Have a choice whether to go or not
  iv. Am not sure about going

c I **should** go to the cinema tomorrow.
  i. Will definitely go
  ii. Would like to go
  iii. Am not sure whether to go or not
  iv. I ought to go but would prefer not to

We also express uncertainty with words like *perhaps*, or *probably*.

2 Read the sentences below and choose the level of certainty they express.

a Aliens **possibly** exist.
  i. Not very likely
  ii. Likely
  iii. Quite likely
  iv. Very likely

b Aliens **probably** exist.
  i. Not very likely
  ii. Likely
  iii. Quite likely
  iv. Very likely

c Aliens **might** exist.
  i. Not very likely
  ii. Likely
  iii. Quite likely
  iv. Very likely

We can combine both types of words.

3 Arrange the following phrases by order of possibility. Put the most certain first.
  i. I might possibly buy a car.
  ii. I would probably have a huge stereo system.
  iii. I could probably own a house.
  iv. I would perhaps live in America.

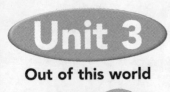

Unit 3
Out of this world
Lesson 7

Assessment Focus
AF3: Organise and present whole texts effectively, sequencing and structuring information, ideas and events
Main text type: Explanation

Student Book pages 68–69

Starter

- Elicit from students the main features of explanation texts (see the list on the next page). Write these up on the board. Then put these two sentences on the board and ask students to confirm which offers an explanation and which offers information.
  - *Orson Wells chooses Mars for his aliens in* The War of the Worlds, *because it clearly has seasons and, it was believed, there was evidence of canals channelling water over its surface.*
  - *Orson Wells wanted a planet where life could exist as his aliens' home planet in* The War of the Worlds. *The planet Mars has seasons and there is some evidence of canals on its surface that might have carried water.*

Introduction

- Introduce the task through the opening panel, and make sure that students have a clear idea of audience as well as format and purpose.

Development

Stage 1
- Students first choose the type of alien they will invent from the options in the bulleted list. Encourage them to be as imaginative as possible with their alien but also make sure that they can give a reason for each of the features they draw. They can also draw on ideas from the text on Student Book pages 63–64. Display **OHT 3.7** and use it to model what they are aiming at.

Stage 2
- Students should refer to the reminder points on the board and in the bullets giving structural guidance (Student Book page 65) as they draft their work. They should be able to state clearly the purpose of each paragraph they are writing – the bullet points can be used as subheadings if necessary.

Stage 3
- Remind students that in this case they need to write in terms of possibilities not certainties and to use some modal verbs. They should also try to include and define some scientific vocabulary and use a range of causal language. It may help to give some examples of causal language in particular next to the reminder point on the board.

Peer Assessment

- When students have completed their writing, ask them to work in pairs, and to read each others' draft explanations. They should check the draft includes the following text-type features:
  - clear, logical organisation
  - precise technical language
  - causal language
  - examples to help explain main points
  - clearly labelled diagrams.
- Ask them to fill in the Peer Assessment Sheet (page 6) and feed back.
- Students redraft their report according to suggestions.

Plenary

- Give a copy of **OHT 3.8** (top half only) to each group and get students to annotate the level 3 writing to show how well it is organised and the range of causal connectives used, and what needs improvement. Then display the whole of **OHT 3.8** and ask for feedback on how to get the level 3 writing up to level 4. Show in the exemplar of level 4 how this can be done. Students make changes to their own texts in light of this.
- Ask 2 or 3 students to read out their explanation texts to the class. Invite the class to give constructive criticism.

Unit 3 — Out of this world

Worksheet 3.7: Gas giant alien

Discuss with a partner why this alien is well suited to living on a gas giant planet. What can you tell about its lifestyle?

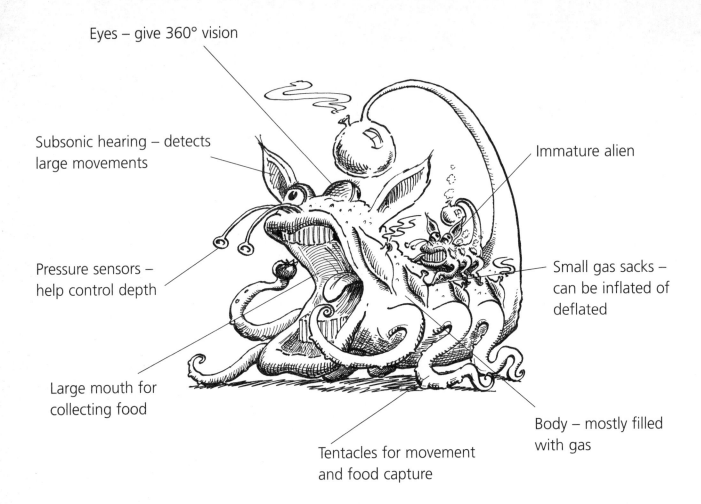

- Eyes – give 360° vision
- Subsonic hearing – detects large movements
- Pressure sensors – help control depth
- Large mouth for collecting food
- Immature alien
- Small gas sacks – can be inflated of deflated
- Body – mostly filled with gas
- Tentacles for movement and food capture

Unit 3 — Out of this world

OHT 3.8: Peer assessment

Assessment Focus

AF3: Organise and present whole texts effectively, sequencing and structuring information, ideas and events

Level 3

This alien is called a hnff. It has big ears and a big nose. It lives on a dark planet. It has four legs and a tail and it is also has another set of arms for holding things.

The planet where it lives does not have much light so there are not many plants for it to eat.

Level 4

Opening sentence gives a clue as to the rest of the paragraph

> This alien is well adapted to a dark planet. It cannot see very well and would use its ears and nose to find things. It feeds off other animals which it hunts. It is called a hnff.
>
> It lives on very dark planet where it is very cold. The alien has very thick fur. It sometimes eats vegetables but these are quite small so it has to eat a lot of them. It has four legs and two tentacles for gripping things.

Facts are backed up by explanations

Good use of causal language

Uses scientific language

A life of crime

Lesson

Framework Objectives

W15: Use a dictionary and a thesaurus with speed and skill

R12: Comment, using appropriate terminology on how writers convey setting through word choice and sentence structure

Wr7: Use a range of narrative devices to involve the reader (withholding information)

Main text type: Narrative

Student Book pages 70–74

 Dictionaries should be available.

Starter

- Discuss simple definitions of a noun, an adjective and a verb. Ask students to identify an example of each in the following sentence from *Holes*:
  A hammock is stretched between the two trees, and a log cabin stands behind that.
- Elicit further alternative examples that might replace them.

Introduction

Key Reading

- Discuss the key features of narrative texts as shown in the text-type box, ensuring students understand by asking the following questions:
  – *What do we learn about the main character from Chapter 1 (for example, age, gender, concerns)?*
  – *What do we call the person who tells the story? Who is this in the extract?*
- Depending on the level of the group, discuss the structure of conventional narrative (i.e. beginning, middle, end), expanding to encompass the stages outlined in the text-type box (i.e. introduction, complication, crisis, resolution).
- Emphasise that the text they are about to read is an 'introduction' (or story opening) and refer to the glossary definitions as you read the *Holes* extract with the class. Once read, ask students what type of opening the extract is. Refer to the examples in the text-type box and reinforce the answer, i.e. 'setting', asking students to use this term in discussion of question **1**. **OHT 4.1** can also be used here.

Development

Purpose

- Students explore the purpose of a story opening through question **3**. Working in groups, encourage them to consider what kind of story opening the text is (i.e. it describes a setting of a desolate nature) and the strengths and weaknesses of different kinds of story openings.
- Conclude work on question **4** by ensuring that students have grasped that the setting is a reform camp and not a summer camp. Explain that the author does not reveal the nature of the camp until Chapter 2, as a device for keeping the reader engaged (withholding information).

Reading for meaning

- Point out the nouns, adjectives and verbs highlighted in the short extract, referring back to the Starter to refresh definitions if necessary. The students may need help in question **5** to replace the adjectives and verbs in the table with suitable ones and should check meanings in a dictionary. Discuss how such choices help to set the tone of the story opening – in particular the use of the verb 'shrivelled' to describe the 'town', 'lake' and 'people' – a skilful device for conveying the sense of desolation felt.

Plenary

- Elicit from the class the main points of a story opening:
  – it can describe a character, setting or event
  – it must engage the reader
  – it can set the tone of the story through its use of language.

Impact English Teacher's Resource © HarperCollins*Publishers* 2005

Unit 4 A life of crime

OHT 4.1: Story openings

1 Identify whether these stories open with:
   – a setting (a place)
   – a character
   – or an event (something happening)?

2 Do any of them focus on more than one feature?

A

Out of the corner of his eye, Keeman noticed a figure enter. He turned to see a man with long black hair, through which ran a silver streak, stride into the middle of the courtyard.

B

A few birds were swirling above the waves, but most had gone. Only the Hurker Rock seemed unimpressed as the storm swept northwards. It was a bleak picture and the coastguard would have its work cut out tonight.

C

"Now I want you all –" Jennifer Jenkins began, but stopped abruptly. A loud noise like the sound of a gun was heard coming from the next room.

D

It was late. Rachel locked the office and walked down the stairs to the street below. As she opened the main door she saw something extraordinary. He was tiny, not more than three years old, and he was sitting with his hands in his lap on the pavement. Rachel looked around her. There was no one else to be seen.

E

"Well, if it wasn't for Angel none of this would have been possible," muttered Josh.
   Angel, thought Becky. I could tell Josh a few things about him. He doesn't know the half of it. But she didn't say a word.

Impact English Teacher's Resource © HarperCollinsPublishers 2005

Unit 4
A life of crime
Lesson 2

Framework Objectives

R8: Infer and deduce meanings using evidence in the text, identifying where and how meanings are implied
Wr5: Structure a story with an arresting opening
Wr14: Describe a setting in a way that includes relevant details and is accurate and evocative
Main text type: Narrative

Student Book pages 74–76

Dictionaries should be available.

Starter
- Draw the distinction between literal information (or information that we can be certain of) and information we infer. Demonstrate this by selecting a student and pointing to something literal about them (for example, what they are wearing). Then compare this with how we might infer what their feelings are by interpreting their facial expressions or body language. Ask students to think of instances where this is tricky – for example, when someone is trying to hide their feelings.

Introduction

Focus on: Knowing and inferring
- Develop from the Starter by referring to the two examples taken from the extract. Ensure students understand they are inferring or 'reading between the lines' in the second example. Ask them to complete question **6** in groups and report back.
- Once you are satisfied they have grasped what inference is, you can broaden the discussion. Encourage students to find clues that indicate what Camp Green Lake is before we are told in Chapter 2, using the examples given. Individuals should then complete the statements in question **7**. (If you introduced the term 'withholding information' in **Lesson 1**, you could ask the class if they can explain its meaning.)

Development

Key Writing
- Students write a story opening in question **8** in which they do not reveal the nature of the setting (a jail/cell) until the last sentence, when they can state the literal truth. The writing should mislead the reader while remaining credible. The focus should be on hidden meanings so that the reader, once they know the truth, should be able to reread the piece and find information that is consistent with the description of a jail. Reinforce this point before the students start.
- Start the exercise by having students assemble appropriate nouns and adjectives to use in their descriptions. The writing frame provided on **Worksheet 4.2** can be used to support less able students in creating a credible description.

Plenary
- Ask 2 or 3 students to read their story openings. The class should decide whether or not they either give too much away to the reader or do not offer a credible description of a jail. Finally, ask students to recall the main points of a story opening as outlined in **Lesson 1**.

Unit 4 A life of crime

Worksheet 4.2: To begin…

Use this frame to help you write your story opening.

1 a Write a few long sentences. Then follow them with one or more short ones. This will vary the pace of your writing.

Although my room…

The walls…

And the floor…

In one corner…

In another corner…

Today I am…

I am thinking…

My door…

The window…

My room…

b Choose from these connectives to make some sentences longer.

| but | like | along with | where |
| when | about | and also | as well as |

_____

_____

_____

_____

_____

Unit 4
A life of crime
Lesson 3

Framework Objective

R7: Identify the main points, processes or ideas in a text and how they are sequenced and developed by the writer

Main text type: Discursive

Student Book pages 77–81

Starter

- Draw a distinction between a fact and a point of view and give some examples. Display **OHT 4.3** and invite the class to identify each statement as a fact or opinion. Ask individuals to provide evidence from each statement to back up their decision. Conclude by asking the class to give their own examples.

Introduction

- Explain that points of view are presented in discursive writing, referring to the definition of the text type provided on page 79. The class can then identify some of the different points of view in the website text during a first read through. Refer to the glossary terms as you read, as some vocabulary (for example, 'distributors') may be outside the students' experience.

Key Reading

- Go through the key features of discursive writing in the text-type box. Check understanding by asking students these questions:
  - Why is the range of views presented in a discursive text?
  - How is each new view signalled?
  - What tense is mainly used in a discursive text?
- Extend question **1** by emphasising that the writer not only presents different views held by different people but also provides evidence of these views. Refer to examples, locating these in the text. Students should note that these are actual quotes, contained within speech marks. Use question **2** to consolidate learning on the use of the present tense.

Development

Purpose

- Introduce the idea that the title of the text can be useful in identifying its main point and that locating key words helps to do this. Question **3a** highlights the fact that the title also includes a pun which helps clarify the main point. Students draw on this and their analysis of the key words in the title to complete a summary of the main point in question **3b** about the opposing points of view involved.

Reading for meaning

- Explain to the class that the opening paragraph in a discursive text usually highlights the main issues. Use the series of bullets to demonstrate that students will need to select the most important point from several being made. In discursive writing key words are often linked (for example, in this case: 'tragedy' and 'focus'). In question **4** students locate the key words in paragraph 2 on their own and explain to a partner how the key words are linked and how paragraph 2 is linked to the previous one.

Plenary

- Elicit from the class the main features of a discursive text. Reiterate them if necessary:
  - it is told in the present tense
  - it links ideas, often using connectives
  - it presents more than one point of view supported by evidence.

Unit 4 A life of crime

OHT 4.3: Point of view or fact?

Decide which of these statements is a point of view and which is a fact.
Which words give you clues?

1. I think too many people are sent to prison.

2. In my view there is more crime than ever.

3. Over 20% of robbery victims are children.

4. The punishment for drivers who break the law is too lenient.

5. Official records say car theft is going down.

6. Young people get blamed too often for the rise in crime.

7. The number of houses being burgled fell dramatically between 1993 and 2001.

8. Thefts *from* vehicles far outnumber thefts *of* vehicles.

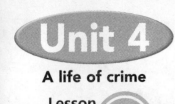

Unit 4
A life of crime
Lesson 4

Framework Objectives

W20: Expand the range of link words and phrases used to signpost texts, including links of cause

R1: Know how to locate resources for a given task, and find relevant information in them (key words)

Wr12: Develop ideas and lines of thinking in continuous text

Main text type: Discursive

Student Book pages 82–83

Starter

- Ask students to define a point of view and explain how they would locate the viewpoints in a text. (They should use the term 'key words'). You can ask them to complete **Worksheet 4.4**. This gives practice in locating facts and opinions quickly in an extract called *The Clink*.

Introduction

Focus on: Points of view

- Students begin by looking at the way Kim Howells' view is expressed, then decide what the main point is. This requires inference. Certain key words such as 'culture' and 'killing' should give clues, along with students' own knowledge of the culture of rap music. Students need to understand which position Kim Howells takes (question **5**) and record his comments (question **6**). The grid provides a systematic way of helping students to identify and record essential information. They can work individually or in groups to complete questions **7** and **8**, reporting back after each example. Round off this section by asking students how balanced the views are, for and against, in the article.

Development

Key Writing

- Before students begin writing, draw together the main points of view recorded in the grids and allow students to express their own points of view on the issue as part of question **9a**. Remind them that when giving their opinion they should provide reasons, linking these with simple connectives such as 'because' or 'so' (rather than merely stating what they believe). For example: *I think that gun crime has risen because…*
  Point out that by giving a reason they are supporting their view effectively.

- More than one view should be exchanged including those that express support for both positions. Remind students that a discursive account looks at an issue from more than one perspective (unlike an argument). Discussing the issue and giving reasons for opinions will also prepare students for completing the writing frame, where they need to present a range of views before concluding with their own.

Plenary

- Invite 2 or 3 individuals to read out their completed frames. Write up any fresh views on the board or OHT and ask students to consider these. (If certain responses are heavily weighted in one direction, remind students that they need to include some from the other perspective.) Once several responses have been read out, the class could then take a vote on the issue.

Unit 4 — A life of crime

Worksheet 4.4: The clink

> This grim museum is a damp and murky dungeon on the south bank of the Thames. It occupies the site of the famous Clink prison which closed down in 1780, a place that must have sent shivers down the spine of anyone who broke the law. And it was easy to break the law in those days. You could find yourself inside for getting into debt or stealing a loaf of bread.
>
> The more criminals in the prison, the better it was for the Bishops of Winchester. They owned the place and made a tidy profit from it too.
>
> It became so well known that 'clink' became a nickname for any prison.
>
> The museum is really a chamber of horrors. Inside is a range of instruments that were used for torture. You can even handle these weird devices. There are also prisoners forever fixed behind the bars of their cells, but these are only wax models – thank goodness.

1 Underline in red the key words that tell you:

  a where the museum is

  b what site it is on

  c when the prison closed

  d a nickname for prisons

  e who owned the prison.

2 Underline in blue the key words that tell you the writer's opinion of:

  a the museum

  b what people must have felt who broke the law

  c the instruments of torture.

Unit 4
A life of crime
Lesson 5

Framework Objectives

- **W16:** Work out the meaning of unknown words using etymology
- **S15:** Vary the formality of language in writing to suit different circumstances
- **R14:** Recognise how writers' language choices can enhance meaning
- **Main text type:** Poetry

Student Book pages 84–88

📖 Dictionaries should be available.

Starter

Key Reading
- Begin by running through the main features of poetry as listed in the text-type box. Note in particular that poetry experiments with all kinds of forms and highlight the shape poem and list poem examples provided. Ask students to identify other forms of poetry. Then see if they have some notion of the form used in *The Trial of Derek Drew*.

Introduction
- Read the poem to the class, without discussing the glossary terms at this stage.
- Go through the key features of poetry in the text-type box. Check understanding by asking these questions:
  - *Have you ever written a shape poem? What shape was it?*
  - *What other kinds of poetry and rhymes do you know?* (for example, haiku, limerick, tongue twister)
- Notice if students picked up sufficient cues from reading the poem to answer questions **1** and **2**. Explain only that much of the vocabulary used in the poem is the language of the law courts. Help students weigh up the differences in the two contexts offered in question **2**.

Purpose
- Once students are sure of the trial context, they can move on to question **3** to consider the humour in the poem. The class should appreciate that this arises from the juxtaposition of the austere language with the triviality of Derek's 'crimes'.

Development

Reading for meaning
- Return to look in greater detail at the legal terms and explain the meanings of the words in the glossary. (Most French-based vocabulary came to us after the Norman Conquest. French had a high status and was the language of the law and administration.) **Worksheet 4.5** offers students the opportunity to study word origins by examining vocabulary from other old languages.
- Discuss the style and structure of the poem, first pointing to the headings above each verse (for example, *The Charges, Also Charged*). Then make sure that students know the difference between formal and informal language, and model one example of each from the poem.
- Having prepared the ground, students can work in groups to answer questions **4**, **5** and **6**, appointing someone to record the answers and another to report back.

Plenary
- Ask groups to feed back their answers to questions **4**, **5** and **6**. Clarify or reinforce points regarding the meaning and effect of repeated words and the informal language used in the poem.

Impact English Teacher's Resource © HarperCollinsPublishers 2005

Unit 4 — A life of crime

Worksheet 4.5: Looking for clues

You can sometimes work out the meaning of a word by studying where it came from. For example, the word 'ascend' comes from Latin:

ad means 'to'

scandere 'climb'

ascend means 'to climb' or 'go up'

1 Work out the modern meaning of these words by studying their origins.

2 Write down your answers in the third column of the chart below.

Word	Origin	Modern meaning
crater	Greek *krater* 'large bowl'	
donate	Latin *donum* 'gift'	
gladiator	Latin *gladius* 'sword'	
gullet	Latin *gula* 'throat'	
mirth	Old English *myrgth* 'merry'	

3 Check your answers in a dictionary that includes word origins.

Framework Objectives

Wr8: Experiment with the visual and sound effects of language

S&L3: Tailor the structure, vocabulary and delivery of a talk or presentation so that listeners can follow it

Main text type: Poetry

Student Book pages 88–89

Starter

- Remind students of the main verse headings in *The Trial of Derek Drew* and elicit examples of formal and informal language used in the poem.
- Explain to students that in this lesson they will write their own poems using a similar structure and present their poems to each other. Whether both tasks are completed in a single lesson will depend largely on how sophisticated the performances are.

Introduction

- The suggestions for verse headings in the Student Book are purposely simpler than those in the poem (i.e. 'The Charges', 'For the Defence', 'The Verdict', 'The Sentence'). If students follow this structure, their poems will be easier to manage. However they could add more headings if they wish, using the courtroom vocabulary they have learned. For example, *Mitigating Circumstances*.

Development

Focus on: Shaping a poem

- Once students are happy with this structure they can begin to add content under each of the four headings as part of questions **7** and **8**.
- Work with a group of students who need extra support in writing in an appropriate style using the writing frame in **Worksheet 4.6**. This supplies more starters under 'The Charges' heading along with one answer under 'For the Defence' (i.e. *I fell asleep*) and further lines. Providing this clear framework should leave students free to concentrate on generating ideas for their poem.

Key Speaking and Listening

- In groups of 3 or 4, students read their poems and decide which one they will perform to the class. Once chosen, it would be best to give students some clear instructions about how to practise a group performance. Along with the prompts given on Student Book page 89, they will need to decide how they are going to position themselves, avert their eyes from the audience and retain composure. Performances can be kept simple by students having only one role each and writing out only their own lines and roles. However, using props (such as chairs or tables) can help students stay in role.

Plenary

- When each group has presented its poem, invite students to assess how well they performed. Emphasise that they should consider both strengths and weaknesses. Ask them to consider the following:
  - how they projected their voices
  - whether they stayed in role
  - whether or not they worked sufficiently well as a team.

Unit 4 A life of crime

Worksheet 4.6: Shaping a poem

The Trial of... _____

[Fill in your name here]

Use the form and ideas below to shape your poem.

- Think of more charges and excuses (under 'Charges' and 'For the Defence').
- Decide what the verdict will be.
- Decide what the sentence will be. (Think of something comic.)

Charges ← [heading]

For leaving my schoolbag on the bus. ← [ideas]
For being late five days in one week.

[Write your ideas here]

For... _____

For... _____

For... _____

For the Defence

I fell asleep.

Day 1   I had to take my sister's dog out

Day 2   It chewed my shoe

[Vary your line lengths]

Day 3   _____ my sock

Day 4   _____

Day 5   _____

[What else can you think of?]

The Verdict

_____

_____

_____

The Sentence

_____

_____

_____

A life of crime

Lesson 7

Assessment Focuses

AF4: Construct paragraphs and use cohesion within and between paragraphs

AF7: Select appropriate and effective vocabulary

Main text type: Narrative

Student Book pages 90–91

Starter

- Explain to students that they are going to write a model narrative, first working out a detailed plan as a guide. They can deviate from the plan if a better idea comes along once they are writing.

Introduction

Stage 1

- Using the example given – a loft in an empty house – brainstorm ideas to help students flesh this out as the setting. These prompts may help to guide the brainstorm:
  - *What does the loft look like?*
  - *How large is it?*
  - *What is in the loft?*
  - *What words describe the atmosphere in the loft, so that the story opens in an exciting or mysterious way?*
- Next, introduce the main character, who is a criminal. Again brainstorm for ideas: character's name, age, main personality traits.

Development

Stage 2

- Once they have an idea of setting and character they can work out a loose plot. Model a spider diagram on the board with students, to explore possibilities using the question prompts supplied. The class could agree on a particular direction to take or individuals may wish to develop their plot ideas in different ways. Refer students who experience difficulties to **Worksheet 4.7**. They can use this to explore two possibilities, choosing one for their plot.

Stage 3

- Again, present the question prompts to help students decide on their resolution. Here they may differ considerably in their ideas for an ending. Guide a group of students in exploring the consequences for their characters of the story endings.

Stage 4

- Help the class construct the opening of the story together, before they work independently to write their stories.

Challenge

- More confident story writers may be able to think of two endings for their story. Show them how to step outside the story as the narrator. Help them to think of questions to ask the reader. Their final story can retain both its endings and a partner could say which they prefer and why in the Peer Assessment.

Peer Assessment

- When students have completed their writing, they work in pairs and read each others' draft narrative. Write up the text-type features listed below and ask pairs to check if their drafts include them.
  - use of narrative structure
  - use of description and dialogue to create characters
  - use of powerful words to make the story more interesting.
- They then fill in the Peer Assessment Sheet (see page 6) and feed back their findings.
- Students redraft according to suggestions.

Plenary

- Give each group a copy of **OHT 4.8** (top half only). Ask students to annotate the level 3 writing to show whether students have used adjectives to add detail, new paragraphs to indicate change of scene and the use of more interesting connectives, as well as what needs improving. Then display the whole of **OHT 4.8** and ask for feedback on how to get the level 3 writing up to level 4. Show in the exemplar of level 4 how this can be done, then get students to make changes to their own texts in light of this.
- Ask 2 or 3 students to read their narratives to the class. Invite constructive criticism from other students.

Unit 4 — A life of crime

Worksheet 4.7: The plot

Below are two courses of action (1 and 2) for your story. Work through each one in your mind first. Then choose one and write your ideas in the boxes.

What happens?

1

Something happens to the character. What?

2

The character finds something in the loft. What?

What are the consequences of this?

What does he/she do next?

Unit 4 — A life of crime

OHT 4.8: Peer assessment

Assessment Focuses
AF4: Construct paragraphs and use cohesion within and between paragraphs
AF7: Select appropriate and effective vocabulary

Level 3

Bilu stood in front of a large door. He turned the wooden handle. The door didn't open. He turned the handle again and pushed the door with his shoulder. The door opened a little and Bilu went into the attic.

There were boxes and cases piled up on the floor. They were covered in cobwebs. In the ceiling was a small skylight.

Level 4

> Bilu stood in front of a large, heavy door. He turned the wooden handle. The door didn't open, so he turned the handle again, pushing with his shoulder. The door opened a little with a creak and Bilu squeezed round it into the attic.
>
> There were lots of boxes and cases, which were covered in cobwebs, piled up on the dusty floor. In the ceiling was a tiny skylight.

Annotations:
- noun phrase developed (→ "large, heavy door")
- connective makes the sentence longer
- more interesting verb replaces 'went'
- phrase adds detail
- clause adds detail

Impact English Teacher's Resource © HarperCollinsPublishers 2005

Unit 5
Drama in the making
Lesson 1

Framework Objectives

R18: Give a considered response to a play as script, focusing on interpretation of action, character and event

S&L15: Develop drama techniques to explore in role a variety of situations and texts or respond to stimuli

S&L16: Work collaboratively to devise and present scripted and unscripted pieces, which maintain the attention of an audience

Main text type: Play script

Student Book pages 92–96

Starter

- Introduce the idea of a 'frozen tableau' – a still picture or statue of an idea, moment, or line created by the students with their own bodies. Then encourage them to form into small groups and create a series of tableaux for the following words: 'family', 'prison', 'illness' and 'brothers'.
- Once each group has decided on their statues/tableaux, ask students to run them as a sequence decided by you (i.e. you could ask for 'family' first). This can be done by individual groups for the class, or as a whole class with each group making the tableau as you say the word. When finished, ask students what 'story' they think is being told in each case.

Introduction

- Ask the same groups to divide up the parts in *Two Weeks with the Queen* and read the extract (with weaker readers taking the shorter parts). Groups need only read, not perform at this stage.

Key Reading

- Run through the key features of drama texts as shown in the text-type box. Check understanding by asking these questions:
  - *How is speech shown in novels and stories?*
  - *What is the purpose of stage directions?*
- Then draw their attention to the issues raised in questions **1** and **2** on page 95, so they clearly make the link between script layout and the extract they have read together.

Purpose

- As a whole class, go through questions **3** to **5**, which encourage students to explore the structure of the play's opening by giving a brief introduction followed by the setting up of two problems. Help them establish what the most important problem will be as the play unfolds.

Development

Reading for meaning

- Students discuss question **6** in pairs, in order to get a sense of the tone of the scene.
- Then they should form into groups and think about how they could represent each of the following lines as tableaux. As one person in the group says the line, so the rest of the group form the statue/tableau. The 'pictures' they create should be bold and grab the audience's attention.

  Queen: *And a very merry Christmas to you all.*
  Colin: *Nobody ever listens to me.*
  Mum: *Colin love, is there something else bothering you?*
  Luke: *Mum. Mum!*

- Once they have devised their tableaux, ask students present them to the class.

Plenary

- Use **Worksheet 5.1** to make notes and reflect on their own tableaux.

Unit 5 Drama in the making

Worksheet 5.1: Tableaux stories

Once you have completed your group performance, complete this table.

Write in <u>exactly</u> what your group did for each line. Include:

- Where people stood
- How they looked
- Expressions on faces, etc.

Line from play	How our group showed this
Queen: And a very merry Christmas to you all.	
Colin: Nobody ever listens to me.	
Mum: Colin love, is there something else bothering you?	
Luke: Mum. Mum!	

Impact English Teacher's Resource © HarperCollinsPublishers 2005

Drama in the making

Lesson

Framework Objectives

R18: Give a considered response to a play as script, focusing on interpretation of action, character and event

S&L15: Develop drama techniques to explore in role a variety of situations and texts or respond to stimuli

Main text type: Play script

Student Book pages 96–98

Starter

- Recap from **Lesson 1**: what is a 'tableau'? What key features have the students learned about playscripts?

Introduction

Focus on: Developing drama techniques

- Ask the class how actors know how to play a character. Talk about how it is, usually, by trying to find out something about the character – i.e. what they are like or what their motivation is (what they want/desire). Tell students they are going to look at the character of Colin in the play, but emphasise that there are lots of possibilities for the way he is played.
- Try question **7** together as a class (what he says/does and what this might mean). Demonstrate, using the work in question **8**, that there are a number of different ways the words 'I know' can be said. Then ask pairs to try out the full line, using the suggestions **a**, **b** and **c**.
- Work on questions **9** and **10**, with groups preparing and performing a short version of lines 10–24. Go round to each group and listen to what they have to say about how to play each part. Encourage them when they make a conscious decision about how to play the parts (for example, *bored, shy, enthusiastic, nervous*), but try to get them to link that decision to the way the character might behave (for example, *fidgeting, looking at the ground, staring wide-eyed*).
- Ask 1 or 2 groups to present their rehearsed readings and invite class comment.

Development

Key Writing

- Model the first part of the next scene, as suggested in question **11**. For example:
    Scene 2
    LUKE   on a stretcher. PARAMEDIC leaning over him.
    COLIN Mum, mum …
    MUM   [*ignoring him*] Say something, Luke.
    DAD   Come on, son … give us a smile.
- Run through the reminder points on page 98 with students to ensure they are clear on how to lay out their script and include stage directions. Model the writing using **OHT 5.2** if more support is required.

Plenary

- Ask 1 or 2 students to read out their scene continuations and invite class comment.

Unit 5 Drama in the making

OHT 5.2: The next scene

	Scene 2
Add a **stage direction** to show arrival or presence of medical staff	*LUKE lying on a stretcher. PARAMEDIC…*
Add something **Colin says** as he looks at what is going on (scared, unsure)	COLIN:
Add **Mum's response** to what she sees, and something about her behaviour	MUM (……………………………………………………):
Add a **comment from Dad** about what is happening	DAD:
Add Mum or Dad's **next action**	*DAD/MUM goes/looks…*
Add a line from the **paramedic**	PARAMEDIC:

How to create a stage design

Drama in the making

Lesson

Framework Objective

S13d: Revise the stylistic conventions of instruction texts
Main text type: Instruction

Student Book pages 99–103

Starter

- Ask the class to identify what area of interest/field these words come from:
  *Downstage   Wings   Front-of-house   Props
  Exit   Cue   Set*
  Note that they are all specialist terms associated with theatre. Make sure students know what each means. Are any used only in the theatre (or other show arena)? If so, which? ('Downstage', 'Front-of-house') The others are all used elsewhere in different contexts. Can students suggest where? (For example, 'wings' = part of a bird/aeroplane.)
- Students can then go on to complete the extension challenge on **Worksheet 5.3**, which offers a similar activity linked to other specialist vocabulary.

Introduction

- Explain to the class that they are going to read a set of instructions to help people doing the job of a stage/set designer. Then read through the text explaining any technical terms that may cause difficulty.

Key Reading

- Work through questions **1** to **5**, and review the key features as described in the text-type box. To check understanding, ask students:
  – Can they think of other instruction texts with similar features?
  – Why do teachers use imperative verbs in lessons?

Purpose

- In response to question **6**, draw out the importance of doing certain things in a logical sequence, in this case, the importance of coming up with a range of ideas before making an informed decision on the best one. Question **7** focuses on the different function of each 'chunk' of text.

Development

Reading for meaning

- Ask students to work in small groups to answer question **8** and briefly feed back responses. They might suggest that it is not relevant for the play to be performed traditionally or that it gives added meaning if a modern setting is used.
- Question **9** requires the group to read the text carefully and look for two key things: *how* the part will be played; and the *reference* (evidence from the extract) to show this. Ensure students are able to pinpoint each reference and write it onto the grid at the bottom of **Worksheet 5.3**.
- Finally, students can prepare the props list for question **10**, which provides good practice in skimming and scanning.

Plenary

- Feed back the information found on the grid for question **9**, and make the students indicate clearly where they found their answer.

Unit 5 — Drama in the making

Worksheet 5.3: Two tasks

1 Group these words into similar sets (that is, as you did for the words connected with the theatre). Some of these might go under *more than one* heading:

corner	line	shot	box	attack	penalty
radius	bomb	spot-kick	number	shell	referee
graph	tank	sum	grenade		

Football match	Maths	War

2

Character	How is he/she played?	Reference from text
Little Red Riding Hood	Little princess	LRRH is like a little princess, lost in her own garden.
Granny		
Wolf		
Woodcutter		

Impact English Teacher's Resource © HarperCollinsPublishers 2005

Unit 5
Drama in the making

Lesson 4

Framework Objectives

S16: Investigate the differences between spoken and written language structures

S&L13: Work together logically and methodically to solve problems, make deductions, share, test and evaluate ideas

Main text type: Instruction

Student Book pages 103–105

Starter

- Ask students about how written and spoken English differ, for example the way we hesitate in speech, rework things as we think, add phrases (*you know*, *actually*, *well*). Also draw attention to times when we need to match more closely what we say to how we write. Why might this be true of instructions? (Because in instructions precision and accuracy are all-important.)

Introduction

Focus on: Working together

- Organise the class in groups of 3 or 4. Then run through question **11**, explaining that in the early stage of planning a stage design for the opening of *Two Weeks with the Queen* the focus will be on how to work best as a group. Ask groups to discuss the three bullet points that give them the basic rules for successful group work – how they can be clear about what they have to do, why the order of tasks is so important, why job division has to be agreed upon.
- Then introduce question **12**, emphasising that students only have to *plan* how they will produce the design for now. Individuals then produce their own plan for how their group would make best use of the two hours available. The process should also be logical – point out to students the idea of generating ideas first, *then* settling on a final choice.

Development

Key Speaking and Listening

- Once students have completed their plan, they can create their own design (question **13a**) for the first scene of *Two Weeks with the Queen*, and then present it (question **13b**).
- Refer students back to **Unit 9** (pages 186–207) for more on effective note-taking. Remind students of the structure of the instruction text on page 101. **Worksheet 5.4** provides a frame for them to work with a similar structure to write up their own notes.
- Give students twenty minutes to complete their plan. Then ask them to present their plans to their original groups. Make them aware that evaluating how they contributed and listened to the discussion is more important than the content itself.
- Students can use **Worksheet 5.4** to record the comments made by the group on the strengths and weaknesses of their plan.

Plenary

- First, each group feeds back briefly on the designs presented and comments made. Then invite groups to talk about how well they worked together. Were they able to contribute and support each other? Challenge them to assess how well they used the rules for successful group work.

Unit 5 — Drama in the making

Worksheet 5.4: Design ideas

Use this sheet to:

- **plan your own individual design** (before you discuss your ideas in a group)

or

- **record your group's ideas** during/after the discussion.

	Your ideas for your design	**Comments from the group**
General description of the stage/set (for example, where furniture, exits, objects would go).		
General mood you want to get across (for example, 'confused and wild', 'calm and peaceful').		
Where the action should take place for the scene you are studying (for example, 'paramedic should enter from behind curtain').		
Any other details you want to mention (for example, sound/music).		

Drama in the making

Lesson 5

Framework Objective

R8: Infer and deduce meanings using evidence in the text, identifying where and how meanings are implied

Main text type: Review

Student Book pages 106–110

Starter

- Organise students in pairs, with one taking on the role of an interviewer and the other of a person being interviewed. The subject of the interview should be any film or TV programme the 'interviewee' has seen. The key here is for the 'interviewer' to find out as much as he/she can about the film/programme and what the interviewee thought of it, by using different types of questions. Encourage each interviewer to ask open questions starting as follows:
  What? How? Why? Where? When? (for example, *So, what happened in… ?*)

Introduction

- Read the film review of *Finding Nemo*.

Key Reading

- Go through the text-type features and check understanding by asking these questions:
  - Has the review provided the 'what', 'how' and 'why' about the film's story?
  - Has it also covered the other 'what' – what the reviewer thinks of the film?
  - Adjectives are added to nouns to create 'noun phrases' like 'a touching film'. Create some simple noun phrases, perhaps about a programme (i.e. a brilliant drama).
- Consolidate this by working through questions **1** to **5**.

Purpose

- Support less able students on question **6** in identifying the 'snapshots' from the film that have been used to tantalise the reader. Ask if they are evenly spaced through the review.
- When looking at question **7**, point out that the writer's opinion isn't always stated obviously. He doesn't have to say, 'I loved this film' because it is clear if he says that it is 'stunning' that this is what he thinks.

Development

Reading for meaning

- Emphasise the importance of the final paragraph of the review in summing up the film. Ask students to complete question **8**, drawing on their close reading for question **6**.
- Then invite students to look at **Worksheet 5.5**, which provides a final paragraph from an alternative review. In small groups students should read and highlight in colour the different sections dealing with:
  - the overall qualities of the film
  - the makers of the film
  - a particular character from the film.
- The group then decides what the reviewer's viewpoint is and provides evidence from the review.

Plenary

- Groups share responses to the **Worksheet 5.5** question, and end by drawing out the ingredients of a good review: the storyline (the who, what, how, why and where) and the reviewer's viewpoint (his/her opinion), ensuring they are clear about how this opinion is conveyed.

Impact English Teacher's Resource © HarperCollinsPublishers 2005

Unit 5 — Drama in the making

Worksheet 5.5: Final paragraph

> Pixar Studios know how to make a hit film, but surely they should now turn their attention to something a bit more grown-up. *Monsters Inc.* worked because it was new, and people were surprised that Pixar could challenge Disney, but *Finding Nemo* doesn't add to Pixar's reputation.
>
> Let's be honest, the vegetarian shark, Bruce, is a joke. OK, he's supposed to be funny, but surely sharks in films are meant to be frightening – what's the point of having them if they're not?
>
> All in all, *Finding Nemo* is a dull film with little to recommend it unless you like the idea of silly little fish talking. Its animations are no more than average and are already looking out of date alongside the fantastic graphics of films such as *Troy* and *The Day After Tomorrow*. The end result is a cute, but rather sentimental film, which doesn't live up to its promise.

1 Look for evidence of:
- the overall qualities of the film (if any)
- the makers of the film
- a particular character from the film.

2 Decide how this reviewer's viewpoint is different from the one in your textbook (page 106–107). Show evidence for this from the text.

Reviewing Nemo

Drama in the making

Lesson

Framework Objectives

S17: Use standard English consistently in formal situations and in writing

S&L17: Extend their spoken repertoire by experimenting with language in different roles and dramatic contexts

S&L19: Reflect on and evaluate their own presentations and those of others

Main text type: Review

Student Book pages 110–112

Starter

- Revise understanding of the idea of a noun phrase. Explain to students that generally this means:

adjective	+	noun
comic		*moments*
fantastic		*story*

  Make the point that these are useful in other sorts of writing (for example, persuasion and information texts), and enable the writer to pack more information into one phrase.

- As a class they can suggest adding simple adjectives to these descriptions (written up on the board):
  - The _____ child ran from the bullies. (for example, *frightened*, *pale*)
  - The bully, a _____ boy of 15, caught up. (for example, *large*, *spotty*)
  - But then a _____ dog raced round the corner. (for example, *enormous*, *snarling*)
  - It belonged to the boy.

Introduction

Focus on: Evaluating spoken presentations

- In question **9**, students work in pairs to complete this spoken task (or as a whole class with teacher as prompt) to suggest phrases based on the examples given (i.e. in the table). Encourage students to think about noun phrases that describe both the plot and the main character(s). Some combinations may sound rather comic or awkward. Ask students to identify these and rework them, for example:

  It features a muscular young detective who is hunting a tall, lonely waitress...

  Students end by giving their overall opinion of the programme/film they have reviewed.

- Pairs/class then feed back on how well the spoken review went in question **10**, using the bullet points on page 112 of the Student Book.

- An extension task is offered on **Worksheet 5.6**, which has transcripts of two people talking about a programme they have seen. Pairs should decide:
  - which of the two speakers tells us more about the characters in the programme
  - where noun phrases have been used.

Development

Key Writing

- Each student then writes the summary paragraph of the review for question **11**. Emphasise that they should include both a summary and their own final opinion, as shown in the writing frame.

Plenary

- Review the students' **Worksheet 5.6** findings, and then listen to examples of review paragraphs. The class should decide which of the summary paragraphs are most effective and why.

Impact English Teacher's Resource © HarperCollinsPublishers 2005

Unit 5: Drama in the making

Worksheet 5.6: *EastEnders* chat

TINA: Did you see *EastEnders* last night?

JO: Yeah, it was well cool. But, I dunno, I still don't know what's going on with Alfie and Kat.

TINA: Basically, he thinks she's a two-faced cow.

JO: That's a bit harsh, isn't it?

TINA: Well, she cheated on him, didn't she?

JO: S'pose so.

TINA: Still, he's not exactly perfect.

JO: I like Alfie.

TINA: So do I. But he's not some innocent saint, is he? I mean, he got the manager's job at the Vic by lying.

JO: Yeah – but that was ages ago. He's good at his job.

TINA: Personally, I think the storylines are just silly. Everyone's a bit dodgy. I mean, anyone would think London's full of shifty crooks!

JO: Yeah, well.

1 Which speaker tells us more about the characters in the programme?

2 Find the noun phrases and underline them.

Unit 5

Drama in the making

Lesson 7

Assessment Focus
AF7: Select appropriate and effective vocabulary
Main text type: Review

Student Book pages 113–115

Starter

- Recap on the key elements of reviews. Elicit as many of the following points as possible from the class before summarising on the board.
  - the *information given* (the who, what, where, when and why)
  - the *viewpoint of the reviewer*, usually given in an entertaining way – either to make us want to see the film, or to point out its faults
  - the use of the *present tense* (especially for film reviews)
  - the *structure* (how many reviews end with a *summary* paragraph).

Introduction

Stage 1
- Take students through the summary notes as listed.

Stage 2
- At the start of Stage 2, invite students to give a verbal opinion about this episode using adjectives from the grid on page 114 of the Student Book. As they do so, they should also add a qualifying adverb from the list below (written up on the board):

  | totally | quite | rather | very |
  | entirely | somewhat | completely | genuinely |

- After each suggestion, ask the class how strong the opinion was, referring to the adverbs used. (NB Take care with 'quite' which can mean 'a little' and 'totally', as in 'it was quite unbelievable'/'she was quite dreadful as an actress' where the stress is put on the 'quite'.)

Development

Stage 3
- Entering Stage 3, students write three 'adjective + noun' combinations on their own to describe three characters.
- Use **Worksheet 5.7**, which provides samples of level 3 and level 4 writing in relation to AF7, to stretch more confident students. Ask them to identify students' writing at the higher levels (students 2, 3, 5 and 7). They should be able to spot students who add to their noun phrases, who add detail in other ways, or who start sentences in more interesting ways.
- Then, using the plan on page 115, students should write their own review of the episode, paying particular attention to the way they expand their sentences to say more about the story or characters. Alongside this they should remember to use the present tense, and use the key elements of review texts.

Peer Assessment

- When they have finished their writing, students work in pairs to read each others draft reviews, and then check they include the following text-type features:
  - key information
  - use of present tense
  - opinion of reviewer
  - final summary paragraph.
- Fill in the Peer Assessment Sheet (page 6) and feed back.
- Students then redraft according to suggestions.

Plenary

- Give a copy of **OHT 5.8** (top half only) to each group and get students to annotate the level 3 writing to show how well the student has selected appropriate and effective vocabulary, and what needs improvement. Then display the whole of **OHT 5.8** and ask for feedback on how to get the level 3 writing up to level 4. Show in the exemplar of level 4 how it can be done. Students make changes to their own texts in light of this.
- Invite 4 of the more confident students to present their reviews to the class, who comment on their strengths and weaknesses. If possible, choose students who have different views on the programme's success.

Unit 5 Drama in the making

Worksheet 5.7: Expanding sentences

These students, writing about an imaginary soap, are writing at level 3 or level 4. Which ones have added information and detail, or started a sentence in an interesting way?

Student 1

In *Dale Street*, Dave Turner is a businessman. He isn't very nice. He can be quite cunning.

Student 2

In *Dale Street*, Dave Turner is a slimy, cunning businessman.

Student 3

Dave Turner lives in a posh, trendy flat in the busy city centre.

Student 4

Dave Turner has a flat. It's in the city centre.

Student 5

By the end of the first episode, we find out what a slimy creep Turner really is.

Student 6

Dave Turner is a creep. He does some bad things at the end of the first episode.

Student 7

Jayne Martin, Dave Turner's ex-wife, is the clear star of the first episode, with her strong, determined personality.

Student 8

Dave Turner's ex-wife Jayne appears in the first episode. She is a strong and determined person.

Unit 5 — Drama in the making

OHT 5.8: Peer assessment

Assessment Focus
AF7: Select appropriate and effective vocabulary

Level 3

This episode of *EastEnders* has us watching with lots of interest. I really wanted to know what happened next. This means what happened to Ian and Dot, and all the others. It was a great episode and you'll be mad to miss it cos it has everything such as excitement and emotion.

Level 4

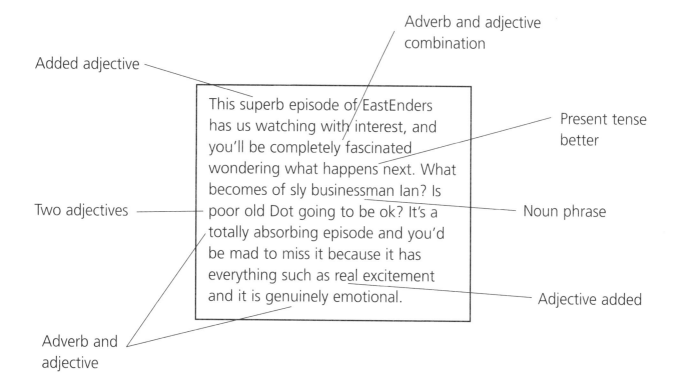

Impact English Teacher's Resource © HarperCollinsPublishers 2005

If a snake bites....

Far from home

Lesson

Framework Objective

S13d: Revise the stylistic conventions of instruction texts
Main text type: Instruction

Student Book pages 116–119

Starter

- Explain to the class that you are going to describe various holiday emergencies. Then ask individual students to shout out what they would say if they were in these situations. For example:
  - *your little brother is about to run across the road*
  - *your friend is wandering off in the jungle*
  - *your mother is in the toilet when the ferry is landing.*
- Write their instructions on the board. Put sentences with imperatives on one side, and those in plain language but without imperatives on the other. Then ask the class what makes the examples in each group similar. Don't use the term 'imperative' at this stage.

Introduction

- Read the leaflet aloud to the class, checking difficult words are understood.

Key Reading

- Run through the key features of instruction texts as shown in the text-type box. Check understanding by asking students these questions:
  - *The bullet points are collected in groups. How many groups are there?* (Three)
  - *Point to two more imperative verbs used in the Starter activity.*
  - *Point to two examples of a plain and simple style used in the Starter activity.*
- Then get students to discuss questions **1** to **3** in pairs. Ask 2 or 3 pairs to feed back their answers and invite the class to comment.

Development

Purpose

- Read the section to the class, and reinforce by referring back to the Starter. Point out the imperatives used at the start of their sentences. Ask 2 or 3 students to reword one of their sentences so that it becomes a less effective general statement (as in the example), and ask what effect this would have had in the scenarios.
- Model the sample sentence in question **4** on the board or OHT before getting pairs to reword the other two. **Worksheet 6.1** provides these and other examples for students who have more time or ability to manipulate.

Plenary

- Invite students to write down three key features of instruction texts without referring to their textbooks and feed back to the class.

Unit 6 Far from home

Worksheet 6.1: Writing instructions

Read the sentences below with a partner, and reword them so that they become short, snappy instructions. The first sentence has been done for you:

1 Sun-tan cream offers protection from the sun for a short time, but you must keep putting it on.

   Keep putting on the sun-tan cream. It only offers protection for a short time.

2 If you don't want to be burnt, you shouldn't stay out in the sun for long periods.

3 Extra care is needed when you visit hot countries like Australia.

4 When you are travelling in these areas, it is not advisable to drink tap water.

5 Using a water-resistant sun-block will help when you spend time at the beach or the pool.

6 Even if it is hot and cloudy, it is still important to use sun-block – you can still get burnt.

Far from home

Lesson 2

Framework Objectives

W18: Understand and use correctly terms of comparison

S&L4: Give clear instructions that are helpfully sequenced, linked and supported by gesture or other visual aid

Main text type: Instruction

Student Book pages 120–122

Starter

- Ask students to suggest different examples of instruction text, such as:
  - *a sign telling you not to cross the railway when the siren sounds*
  - *a leaflet telling you what to do if you smell gas.*

  Invite 3 students to point to three key instruction text features of the text on page 116 and 117 to remind the class of the text they are studying in this lesson.

Introduction

Reading for meaning

- Work through questions **5** and **6** as a whole class. In question **5** you could ask why reasons may be given (to explain the advice). Then get pairs to work on questions **7** and **8**, focusing particularly on the layout features the writer has used to signal each new instruction. Ask 2 or 3 pairs to feed back their answers.

Focus on: Comparative adverbs

- Read through the explanation of adverbs with the class. Ensure that they understand what a simple adverb is by asking them to supply further examples. Point out that most adverbs end in '–ly', although some common ones are irregular, for example, 'well' as in 'well done'.
- As the comparative function is clearer when the adverb is used with the conjunction 'than', supply an example of this type on the board, alongside the example in the book. For example: *Greg speaks more quickly <u>than</u> Lisa.*
- Ask pairs to copy out the sentences in question **9** and to underline the adverb, and then extend them by choosing the appropriate second clause from the three provided. Ask them to identify the conjunction that links the two clauses in each new sentence.

Development

Key Speaking and Listening

- Students attempt question **10** in groups of 3. Read the instructions to the class before giving each group a copy of **Worksheet 6.2**. Model how pilots would use a pencil to mark their route from London to Paris, for example.
- Suggest different ways in which the controller can indicate direction (or ask students for suggestions), for example, using the compass points and the map scale. Emphasise that the observer's role is to check that the pilot is following instructions exactly, and to suggest ways of improving the air traffic controller's instructions.
- Suggest three different destinations for each group. Make the destinations further afield for abler groups. The air traffic controller chooses which one to guide the pilot to. Support less able groups by acting as their observer for one destination.

Plenary

- Ask 2 or 3 groups to share their experience. What problems occurred? How were they resolved? Then get individuals to jot down their best instruction and to highlight key features that made it a good instruction. Ask 2 or 3 students to feed back.

Unit 6 Far from home

Worksheet 6.2: Giving clear instructions

Listen carefully to the instructions given by your air traffic controller. Then guide your plane to the destination given to you. Use a pencil to mark your route.

You must follow the instructions exactly, as you cannot use your plane's computer or see where you are going.

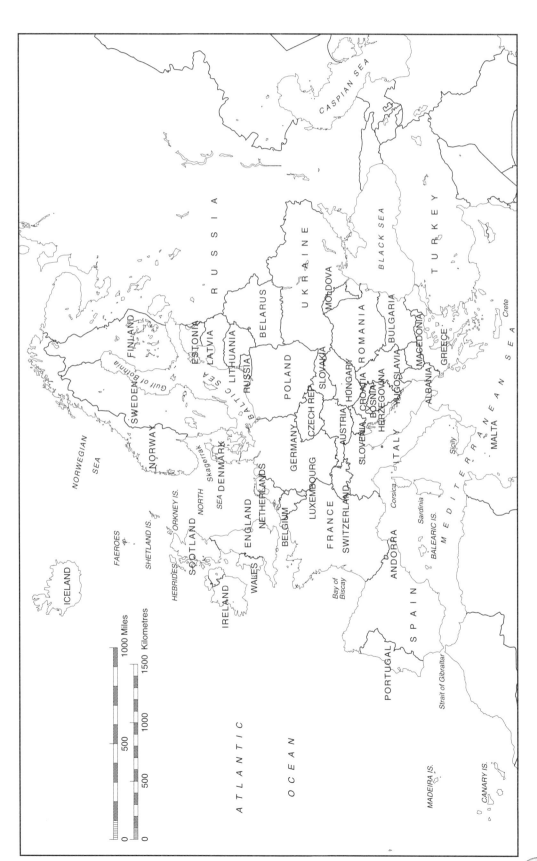

Impact English Teacher's Resource © HarperCollinsPublishers 2005

Far from home

Lesson 3

Framework Objective

S13a: Revise the stylistic conventions of information texts
Main text type: Information

Student Book pages 123–128

Starter

- Brainstorm different information texts that relate to the theme of travel, for example: *a travel brochure, guidebook, children's information book, map* or *timetable*. You could do this orally or build up a spidergram on the board, with 'Travel information' in the centre.
- Ask students what language features many of these texts may share. Do not comment too much on their responses at this stage as this activity is intended as preparatory.

Introduction

- Read the two Brazil texts aloud to the class, checking that the words in the glossary are understood.

Key Reading

- Go through the key features of information texts as shown in the text-type box. Check understanding by asking students these questions:
  - *How many paragraphs has the writer of Text 2 used?*
  - *Find another example of the present tense in Text 2.*
  - *Find two specialist terms that relate to Geography in Text 1.*
- Then get students to discuss questions **1** to **3** in pairs. Invite 2 or 3 pairs to feed back their answers and get the class to comment. More able students could annotate a copy of Text 2 on **Worksheet 6.3** to bring out all examples of the three main features of information texts. Display **Worksheet 6.3** as an OHT and allow students to present their findings to the class.

Development

Purpose

- Read the section to the class, ensuring that students understand what nouns and pronouns are. A noun phrase is simply a group of words that acts as a noun, i.e. it is the subject of the verb in the sentence. Initially, you can show this on the board by starting with a sentence with a simple noun, for example: *The plane*. Then gradually add to it to form a very long noun phrase, such as: *The enormous white British Airways plane standing on the runway was about to take off*.
- Then run through the example sentence from Text 2 and ask pairs to answer question **4** and feed back to the class. Pairs could annotate the relevant sentences in Text 2 on **Worksheet 6.3**, following the model provided.

Reading for meaning

- In question **5**, students practise finding information and evidence from the text by answering questions about football based on Text 2. Question **6** deals with the organisation of the text.

Plenary

- Elicit from students three key features of information texts and reinforce any of these as necessary.

Unit 6 Far from home

Worksheet 6.3: Information texts

Annotate Text 2 to show the main features of information texts. Some of the annotations have been done for you.

present tense

Clear plain statement

This section is all about football. That is why it has been given a paragraph to itself.

scrub dry area of stunted trees and bushes
iron ore iron in its natural form in the ground
minerals inorganic substance found in the ground, for example metals and salts

Brazil

Brazil is the largest country in South America. This huge territory covers nearly half the continent; it is almost as big as the USA. In the west are the foothills of the massive Andes mountains. To the east lie the beautiful beaches on the coast of the vast Atlantic ocean. However, even though it is a large country, a lot of Brazil is hard to access. The north-eastern corner of the country is dry and made up mostly of thorny scrub. The Amazon basin also has a very small population. Most Brazilians live in the cities – the three biggest cities are Sao Paolo, Brasilia (the capital) and beautiful Rio de Janiero. Rio is famous for its colourful annual carnival. Brazilians are a vibrant mixture of races and cultures and this is reflected in their music, dance and art.

Brazil is one of the biggest producers of coffee in the world. Another important export is citrus fruit. Cattle, pigs and sheep are the most common livestock and there are also large deposits of iron ore and other minerals. Brazil is one of the ten biggest industrial nations in the world, but millions of people are poor, while only a few are very wealthy.

The national sport in Brazil is football (or *futebol* as Brazilians call it). They are the only nation to have won the World Cup four times (1958, 1962, 1970 and 1994) and are known to play the most creative and exciting style of the game. Brazilians are passionate about football – it is played all year round, and on big international game days, no one goes to work. Brazil's most famous player is Pelé, who retired in 1977. He scored over 1,000 goals in his 22-year career, and is known in Brazil as O Rei (the king).

Impact English Teacher's Resource © HarperCollinsPublishers 2005

Far from home

Lesson 4

Framework Objectives

R3: Compare and contrast the ways information is presented in different forms

S&L7: Answer questions pertinently, drawing on relevant evidence or reasons

Main text type: Information

Student Book pages 128–129

Starter

- Elicit from the class what the word 'evidence' means. Ask the class various simple questions, for example: *What is Greg's surname?*, and follow each one up by asking what the evidence is for their answer. End by displaying **Worksheet 6.3** as an OHT and ask one or two questions about Text 2, where the evidence also lies in the text. Ask students to come up to the front of the class and point to the evidence for their answers.

Introduction

Reading for meaning

- Read through question **7** and get pairs to conduct the quiz.
- Guide a group of lower ability students in framing questions about Texts 1 and 2. Get them to think about how to make their question clear but without giving away too many clues. Use the example provided in the Student Book as a model for this.
- After the quiz, ask for feedback on the different ways in which those answering indicated evidence, for example, *by pointing to the answer in the text, by referring the questioner to the relevant section/paragraph, by reading out the relevant sentence, etc.*

Focus on: Presenting the information

- Introduce question **8**, explaining that groups are going to analyse the way information on Brazil is presented in Texts 1 and 2. Present **Worksheet 6.4** as an OHT and show how the completed entries make comments on the effects of the features. Invite the class to evaluate how effective they are. Hand out a copy of **Worksheet 6.4** to each group of 4 and ask them to discuss and complete the grid. Circulate around the groups to ensure they evaluate the features as well as simply recording them.
- Ask 2 groups to present their findings to the class, each using their completed worksheet in the form of an OHT. Then in question **9** ask the whole class whether the differences found relate to the different purposes of the texts, giving evidence for their answers. It may help to bring out the difference in the audiences of Texts 1 and 2 to help inform discussion of purpose, i.e. Text 2 is for children, whereas Text 1 is more likely to be for adults.

Development

Key Writing

- Students attempt question **10** on their own. Read Text 1 to the class before they begin work on Text 2, and show how the two sub-headings help to make sense of the note-like information. Students could use their ICT and design skills by using a computer to type up their fact file.

Plenary

- Ask 3 or 4 students to present their fact files and invite comment from the class as to whether they make good clear information texts. Do they differ from each other, and if so, in what ways?

Unit 6 Far from home

Worksheet 6.4: Presentation

In groups, complete the table below to compare and contrast how information is presented in the texts on Brazil. Include any thoughts that you have on the effect of each feature.

	Web page	Encyclopaedia entry
Design/layout Comments on…		
Use of bold/italic and colour	Bold used to show the subheadings – simple but clear. Colour to mark the main heading, and the hyperlinks – makes them stand out.	Bold used for title only. Could do with some more bold to highlight main words?
The size and style of the typeface		
The illustrations		
Headings and subheadings		
Language and style Comments on…		
Length of sentences		
Use of paragraphs	No paragraphs, as text is made up of notes.	3 paragraphs, because dealing with 3 topics. This helps the reader follow the text.

Far from home

Lesson

Framework Objectives

S4: Keep tense usage consistent, and manage changes of tense so that meaning is clear

R6: Adopt active reading approaches to engage with and make sense of texts

Main text type: Recount

Student Book pages 130–134

Starter

- Write six simple sentences on the board that include verbs in different tenses (for example, *I ran home, He is walking quickly*) so that students can identify them. Remind them that in general, verbs describe actions, and that they make sense if you put 'I', 'he' etc. in front of them. Then ask what the tense of a verb tells us (whether it refers to the past, present or future), and get students to identify the tenses of the six verbs. You could end by asking students how they can tell the tense of a verb. Model an example, such as how the past tense is often signalled by verbs ending in '–ed'.

Introduction

- Read the Bill Bryson text aloud to the class, checking the glossary terms are understood.

Key Reading

- Go through the key features of recount texts as shown in the text-type box. Check understanding by asking students these questions:
  - How can you tell that 'arrived' is in the past tense? (Refer back to the Starter if necessary.)
  - Give three examples of time connectives, for example 'until', 'when', 'next'.
  - How many paragraphs are there in the whole passage?
- Then get students to discuss questions **1** to **3** in pairs. Ask 2 or 3 pairs to feed back their answers and get the class to comment.

Development

Purpose

- To put this section in context, ask students to brainstorm different types of recount texts. Write them on the board. Then ask which ones aim to entertain the reader as much as to recount events.
- Students answer question **4** in pairs before feeding back to the class. Remind them to find evidence for their views on each feature that makes the text entertaining.

Reading for meaning

- In question **5**, students discuss the who, what, where, when and why of the text in pairs. They complete question **6** on their own, using **Worksheet 6.5** to highlight the phrases describing the rain. This can then be used as an OHT to present their findings to the class.

Plenary

- Elicit from students the three key features of recount texts, reinforcing understanding of these as necessary.

Unit 6 Far from home

Worksheet 6.5: The rain

Reread the extract looking for references to do with the rain.

1 Write down six words or phrases that refer to the rain.

2 Highlight the verbs, nouns and adjectives in three different colours on your list.

3 Which is the best word or phrase, in your opinion? Follow the example show below.

Adjective and noun – shows the power of the rain: not just a shower.

Bournemouth in the rain

And so to Bournemouth. I arrived at five-thirty in the evening in a driving rain. Night had fallen heavily and the streets were full of swishing cars, their headlights sweeping through bullets of shiny rain. I'd lived in Bournemouth for two years and thought I knew it reasonably well, but the area around the station had been extensively rebuilt, with new roads and office blocks and one of those befuddling networks of pedestrian subways that force you to surface every few minutes like a gopher to see where you are.

By the time I reached the East Cliff, a neighbourhood of medium-sized hotels perched high above a black sea, I was soaked through and muttering. The one thing to be said for Bournemouth is that you are certainly spoiled for choice with hotels. Among the many gleaming palaces of comfort that lined every street for blocks around, I selected an establishment on a side-street for no reason other than I rather liked its sign: neat capitals in pink neon glowing through the slicing rain. I stepped inside, shedding water, and could see at a glance it was a good choice – clean, nicely old-fashioned, attractively priced, and with the kind of warmth that makes your glasses steam and brings on sneezing fits. I decanted several ounces of water from my sleeve and asked for a single room for two nights.

'Is it raining out?' the reception girl asked brightly as I filled in the registration card between sneezes and pauses to wipe water from my face with the back of my arm.

'No, my ship sank and I had to swim the last seven miles.'

'Oh, yes?' she went on in a manner that made me suspect she was not attending to my words closely. 'And will you be dining with us tonight, Mr –' she glanced at my water-smeared card ' – Mr Brylcreem?' I considered the alternative – a long slog through stair-rods of rain – and felt inclined to stay in. Besides, between her cheerily bean-sized brain and my smeared scrawl, there was every chance they would charge the meal to another room. I said I'd eat in, accepted a key and drippingly found my way to my room.

From *Notes from a Small Island* by Bill Bryson

Far from home

Lesson 6

Framework Objective

S8: Recognise the cues to start a new paragraph and use the first sentence effectively to orientate the reader

Main text type: Recount

Student Book pages 134–135

Starter

- As a way of recapping the text, encouraging students to engage with the story, and preparing them for the writing assignment in the last part of the lesson, ask groups to spend two to three minutes discussing how they think the story may continue (question **7**). Then ask for feedback, and write their ideas on the board in the form of a spidergram.

Introduction

Focus on: Structuring a recount text

- Remind students of the text skeleton for recount texts which they will be familiar with from History as a timeline. Construct a simple example on the board first by asking a student to recount what they did at the weekend. Run through the model timeline provided for the text and ask students to copy and complete it for question **8** on their own or in pairs.
- Emphasise the importance of paragraphs as a structural tool, and ensure students know that a new paragraph starts on a new line. Question **9** asks students in groups to think about when it is appropriate to begin a new paragraph, and how the paragraph focus is signalled to the reader. Model the example provided from the extract. Then guide a small group of less able students in discussing the signals given in each paragraph of the main topic.
- To extend this learning, hand out a copy of **Worksheet 6.6** to the same groups and ask them to mark where the new paragraphs should begin. Those who finish first can also highlight the topic sentences on the worksheet. Invite 1 or 2 groups to feed back on their decisions.

Development

Key Writing

- Students attempt question **10** on their own. Remind students of the suggestions for possible continuations of the recount from the Starter. Supply others if necessary, such as the writer flooding the bedroom while running the bath, or get groups to brainstorm possibilities.
- Talk through reminder points, emphasising in particular the fact that each of their two to three paragraphs should have a clear focus and be linked by time connectives. Encourage them to include some dialogue and powerful description to add interest and entertainment value.

Plenary

- Ask 3 or 4 students to present their recounts and invite comment from the class. Look out for the consistent use of the first person, the correct use of tense and the presence of the three features of entertaining writing, as listed on page 135.

Unit 6 Far from home

Worksheet 6.6: Paragraphs

In pairs, read the recount text below. The writer has forgotten to use paragraphs. Discuss where each new paragraph should be (there are four) and mark it on the text. Be ready to present your ideas to the class.

Sir Ranulph Fiennes was born on March 7th 1944, shortly after his father was killed in action during World War II. After the war his mother moved the family to South Africa, where Ranulph lived until he was 12. After school in Britain he served eight years in the British army, followed by service in the private army of the Sultan of Oman. Ranulph has been an explorer and adventurer since the 1960s. He led hovercraft expeditions up the White Nile in 1969, but he completed his most famous trek in 1979–1982, when he and Charles Burton travelled round the world, from pole to pole, using only surface transport. They covered 52,000 miles and became the first people to have visited both poles. In 2000 Ranulph tried to walk on his own to the north pole. However, his sleds fell through the ice and he had to pull them out by hand. This led to severe frostbite in his fingertips, and he had to abandon the expedition. Back at home, Ranulph cut off his dying fingertips with an electric saw in his garden shed. Four months after a heart operation in 2003, Ranulph bounced back to run seven marathons in seven days, one on each continent of the world. The first race, on 26th October, was in South America; the final race, on 1st November, was in North America. The most difficult race was in Singapore, Asia.

Unit 6 Assignment

Far from home

Lesson

Assessment Focuses

AF3: Organise and present whole texts effectively, sequencing and structuring information, ideas and events

AF4: Construct paragraphs and use cohesion within and between paragraphs

Main text type: Information

Student Book pages 136–137

Starter

- Ask students to jot down three main features of information texts, then feed back to the class. Read through the assignment introduction ('Your task') and ask students how the main features they have explored relate to the specific task of writing a factual introduction to a travel guide. For example, if they have said 'present tense', give them alternative sentences on the board (*Greece was a country in Europe/Greece is a country in Europe*) to choose the correct one.

Introduction

Stage 1

- Read through Stage 1 of the assignment and then ask small groups to work out which set of notes (A, B or C) belongs with which topic heading (natural features, general information, tourist attractions). Invite 1 or 2 groups to feed back to the class, so that everyone is on the right lines.

Stage 2

- Groups discuss which order the paragraphs should go in at this stage. In the feedback, emphasise the fact that in information texts the general information usually comes first.

Development

Stage 3

- Students now work on their own to produce individual pieces of writing. Model on the board how you would begin turning notes B into a paragraph of text. Read through the reminders. Guide a group as they compose their information texts. Praise use of powerful nouns or verbs, but do not make this a requirement at this stage.
- Students can practise identifying good paragraph starters if you give pairs the cards on **Worksheet 6.7**. Their task is to group possible paragraph starters under each category card (natural features, general information, tourist attractions); there are three of each. Then they should assess which is the best paragraph starter in each category, using the criteria outlined on page 137 of the Student Book, i.e. using the present tense, clear and precise factual writing and signalling the focus of the paragraph clearly. Get students to justify their decisions in each case, and identify what is wrong with the other starters provided.

Peer assessment

- When students have completed their writing, they work in pairs and read each other's draft recounts. Write up the text-type features listed below and ask pairs to check if their drafts include them.
    - use of present tense
    - use of new paragraph to show new focus
    - precise and sometimes technical vocabulary.
- They then fill in the Peer Assessment Sheet (see page 6) and feed back their findings.
- Students redraft according to suggestions.

Plenary

- Give a copy of **OHT 6.8** (top half only) to groups and get students to annotate the level 3 writing to show how good the cohesion and signalling in the paragraphs is, and what needs improvement. Then display the whole of **OHT 6.8** and ask for feedback on how to get the level 3 writing up to level 4. Show in the exemplar of level 4 how it can be done. Students make changes to their own texts in light of this.
- Ask 2 or 3 students to read their texts to the class and invite constructive criticism from other students.

Unit 6 Far from home

Worksheet 6.7: Paragraph starters

Natural features	General information	Tourist attractions
Greece is a mountainous country.	80% of the land, or nearly 80% – which is almost all of it – is mountains.	When you go to Greece you will see there are lots of islands there.
Greece is a country in south-east Europe.	Although the official name of Greece is the Hellenic Republic, we usually call the country Greece.	Greece is in south-east Europe, on the Mediterranean Sea, with an area of 132,000 sq. km and its capital is Athens.
Greece has a lot to offer the tourist.	Tourism is huge in Greece, lots of people go there every summer because of the weather and seaside.	Also, summer time in Greece is hot and dry.

Unit 6: Far from home

OHT 6.8: Peer assessment

Assessment Focuses

AF3: Organise and present whole texts effectively, sequencing and structuring information, ideas and events

AF4: Construct paragraphs and use cohesion within and between paragraphs

Level 3

… Greece is made up of lots of islands – over 1400 islands in fact. You may want to visit one of them as a tourist, because lots of tourists do. The summer is popular because the summers are hot and dry.

Back to the geography of the country – nearly 80% of the country is made up of mountains or hills. It is very mountainous. There are lots of beaches as well. Tourists love them.

Level 4

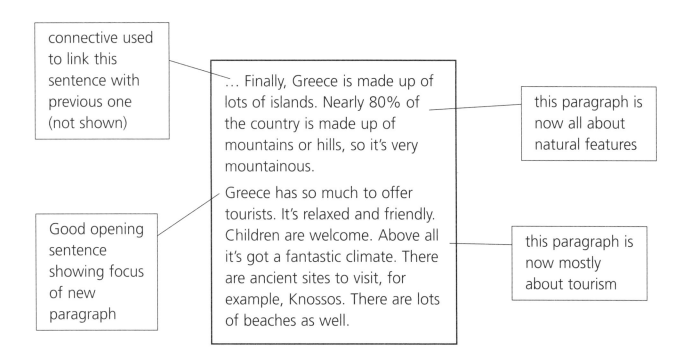

connective used to link this sentence with previous one (not shown)

… Finally, Greece is made up of lots of islands. Nearly 80% of the country is made up of mountains or hills, so it's very mountainous.

this paragraph is now all about natural features

Good opening sentence showing focus of new paragraph

Greece has so much to offer tourists. It's relaxed and friendly. Children are welcome. Above all it's got a fantastic climate. There are ancient sites to visit, for example, Knossos. There are lots of beaches as well.

this paragraph is now mostly about tourism

Impact English Teacher's Resource © HarperCollinsPublishers 2005

Media today

Lesson 1

Framework Objectives
R11: Recognise how print and images combine to create meaning
S13e: Revise the stylistic conventions of persuasion texts
Main text type: Persuasion

Student Book pages 138–142

Recent print adverts with strong image-to-text links.

Starter

- Brainstorm as a class different kinds of adverts, listing the types on the board in the form of a spidergram. Include different media, such as radio, TV and print, and their different purposes/contexts, such as 'for sale' notices or billboards.
- Then invite groups to discuss any memorable adverts they have seen or heard recently, and draw up a short list of features that make them effective. Feed back to the class, listing the main features mentioned on the board, for example, *image, music, story, words*.

Introduction

- Read through and look at the adverts together, ensuring that students understand the terms in the glossary.

Key Reading

- Go through the key features of persuasion texts as shown in the text-type box. Check students' understanding by asking these questions:
  – Do adverts that are mainly pictures also make 'a series of points'?
  – How does the Wall's advert add a reference to sound (see main text at the top)?
  – How is the example given ('… sh-sh-shudder as sharks pass within inches') suggestive?
- Then ask students to discuss questions **1** to **3** in pairs. Ensure they understand what a slogan is first, by providing other well-known examples. Ask 2 or 3 pairs to feed back their answers and invite the class to comment.

Development

Purpose

- Pairs discuss questions **4** and **5** and feed back. Emphasise that the main purpose of an advert is to sell something (even an idea), despite anything else the advert may contain (information or advice, perhaps).

Reading for meaning

- Run through the first half of this section, which illustrates how to 'read' the design components of the Wall's advert. Question **6** asks pairs to analyse the design of the Sea Life Centre advert in the same way. Ensure their analysis focuses on the design of the text/slogans, not the words used. Hand out copies of **Worksheet 7.1** to each pair for them to complete the annotations.

Plenary

- Invite 2 or 3 pairs to present their analysis of the Sea Life Centre advert. Ask the rest of the class to consider:
  – how persuasive the visual images of the Sea Life Centre advert are
  – how persuasive the students' presentation is.

Unit 7 Media today

Worksheet 7.1: 'Reading' the design

In pairs, discuss how effective the design of the Sea Life Centre advert is. Make comments in the boxes below.

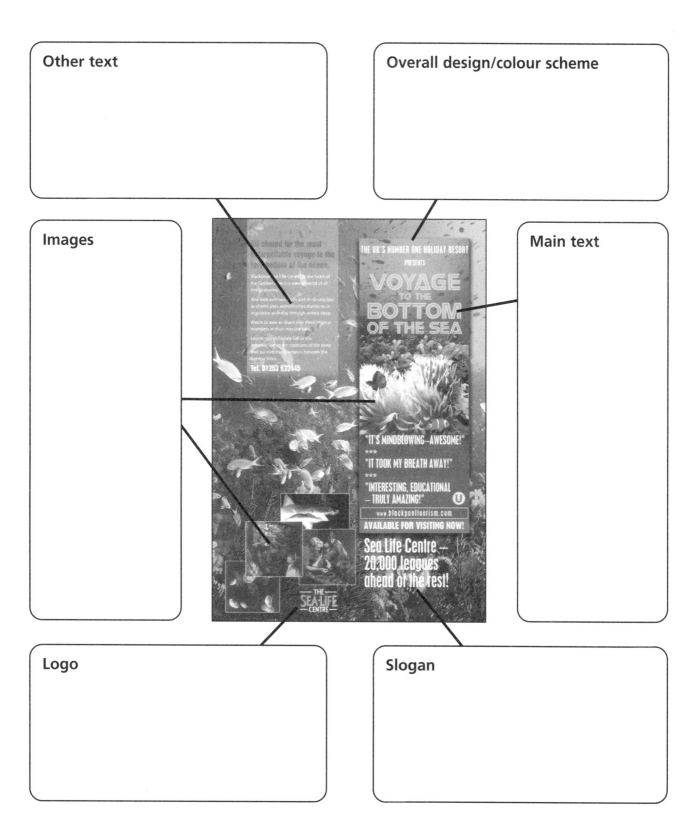

Other text

Overall design/colour scheme

Images

Main text

Logo

Slogan

Impact English Teacher's Resource © HarperCollinsPublishers 2005

Unit 7
Media today
Lesson 2

Framework Objectives

S&L5: Promote, justify or defend a point of view using supporting evidence, example and illustration which are linked back to the main argument

S&L8: Identify the main methods used by presenters to persuade

Main text type: Persuasion

Student Book pages 142–144

 Short clip from a news programme.

Starter

- Show the class a short clip of a practised public speaker in action, such as a politician or a news presenter. Brainstorm the ways in which the speech was presented effectively, focusing on the presentation (*body language, tone of voice, pace of speech, eye contact, confidence, volume*) rather than the words used. Then write a shortlist of the main points on the board under the heading 'Delivering a speech'. Explain that this will act as preparation for the 'Key Speaking and Listening' activity later in the lesson.

Introduction

Focus on: Colourful and suggestive words

- Run through the explanation with the class, emphasising that the text is now the centre of attention. Ensure that they understand what 'emotive' and 'suggestive' mean by providing further examples. Focus on the three bulleted features, then read through the analysis of the Wall's advert and show how each highlighted example is one of the three features already discussed. Ask students how effective they think each example is, giving reasons.
- Groups then analyse the text of the Sea Life Centre advert in the same way for question **7**, completing the grid supplied. Guide a group of lower-ability students in selecting particular words and phrases and commenting on their effect. Invite 2 or 3 groups to present their grids on an OHT for class comment.

Development

Key Speaking and Listening

- Explain question **8**, as outlined. In the same groups, students choose to criticise or praise the Sea Life Centre advert, which has been the focus of their work in the last two lessons. Give each group a copy of **Worksheet 7.2**, which supplies a speaking frame with the topics to cover and possible sentence openers. They will need to adapt the sentence openers to suit their viewpoint and can use the frame as a prompt when making their presentation.
- Emphasise the fact that their presentation has to be persuasive – like the adverts. Remind students of the main features of a persuasion text, and of the shortlist of points for delivering a speech drawn up in the Starter.

Plenary

- Ask 2 or 3 groups to present their case, using a copy of **Worksheet 7.1** as an OHT. The rest of the class should identify the main techniques of persuasion used by the presenters in their delivery, rather than evaluating the content of their presentation.

Unit 7 Media today

Worksheet 7.2: Evaluating an advert

Use the speaking frame below to help with your presentation on the Sea Life Centre advert. Change the suggested sentence openers if they do not suit your point of view.

	Suggested sentence openers
Introduction	We are going to try to persuade you that… The purpose of the advert is …
Design	The design of the advert… The colour scheme is also effective… The photographs all suggest… Different sizes of text have been used… The logo and slogan are at the bottom because…
The words	The writing is packed full of colourful words and phrases, such as… but… 'Sh-sh-shudder' is especially good because… The use of the film title is brilliant: it suggests… Direct address, such as…
Conclusion	So we hope you'll agree that… Isn't this enough to persuade you that…

Impact English Teacher's Resource © HarperCollinsPublishers 2005

Unit 7
Media today
Lesson 3

Framework Objective
S13e: Revise the stylistic conventions of argument texts
Main text type: Argument

Student Book pages 145–148

Starter

- Brainstorm different argument texts. You could do this orally or build up a spidergram on the board, with 'Argument' in the centre. Ask students what language features these texts may share. Do not comment too much on their responses at this stage: this activity is intended as preparatory.

Introduction

- Read the newspaper article aloud to the class, ensuring that students understand the terms in the glossary.

Key Reading

- Go through the key features of argument texts, as shown in the text-type box. Check understanding by asking students these questions:
  – *Why is it important for argument texts to be logical?*
  – *What effect does using evidence have on an argument?*
  – *Why is formal language suited to argument texts?*
- Explain the term 'logical' to the class to inform their analysis of the argument text. Then invite students to discuss questions **1** to **3** in pairs. Ask 2 or 3 pairs to feed back their answers and invite the class to comment.

Development

Purpose

- Pairs first discuss what the writer's point of view is, and what main point she is making. Then they share their responses on the purpose of the text as a class.
- Emphasise that questions **4** to **6** ask them to find examples of the three different methods of backing up an argument to fulfil its purpose.
- As an extension to this, hand out cut-out versions of the cards on **Worksheet 7.3** to each pair, to match each method to the right example sentence (There are two sentences for each method. The three method cards have black backgrounds.). Tell the class that this activity relates to a different text, arguing that television is bad for you. If time allows, pairs can complete each sentence to show how they would win the audience over in different ways.

Plenary

- Ask students to write down three key features of argument texts, reinforcing these as necessary.

Unit 7 Media today

Worksheet 7.3: Television is bad for you

The evidence is clear…	Plenty of studies have shown the bad effects of television…
I only have to look at my own daughters slumped on the sofa…	It is bad for you in several different ways…
When I was a child…	For example, it kills conversation…
evidence/reasons	**personal experience**
examples/further detail	

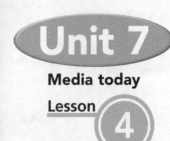

Unit 7
Media today
Lesson 4

Framework Objective
S10: Recognise how sentences are organised in a paragraph in which the content is not chronological
Main text type: Argument

Student Book pages 149–151

Starter

- Ask students what a paragraph is. If necessary, use an example paragraph from the text on pages 145–146 to prompt the discussion.
- After discussion, write up the class definition on the board. Compare it with the definition given on page 150 of the Student Book.

Introduction

Reading for meaning

- Begin this section by running through the features of conversational language in the 'Grammar for reading' box. Then ask individuals to write answers to questions **7** to **9**. If necessary, support question **9** by giving a few prompts on why the final paragraph is an effective ending, for example, *the use of humour, the final line is the same as the title*. Ask 2 to 3 students to feed back and discuss as a class.

Focus on: Organising paragraphs

- Read through the section and show how the sentences in the example paragraph go together. Refer back to work done in the Starter to remind students of the main purpose of organising writing in paragraphs.
- Pairs analyse paragraph 4 in question **10**, looking at how other sentences in the paragraph back up the main point. In question **11**, students analyse paragraph 3 in the same way, working in pairs. Ask 2 or 3 students to present their findings to the class, and ask for class comment.

Development

Key Writing

- Students attempt question **12** on their own. Selecting two main points from the list provided, they write two short paragraphs arguing that toy advertising should not be banned. Emphasise that they will need to open with a sentence or a question that gives their overall view and then back up their main points with examples. The writing frame in **Worksheet 7.4** can be used to support this task. Guide a group of lower-ability students, helping them to select convincing examples to back up their points and to use formal language.

Plenary

- Ask students to write down one sentence describing how this lesson has been useful. They then add a sentence to back up their main point. Ask several students to feed back and invite the class to comment on whether they have written an effective argument. What kind of back-up sentences have been used?

Unit 7 – Media today

Worksheet 7.4: Toy advertising on TV

Use the writing frame below to help you draft your argument on why toy advertising on TV should not be banned.

1st paragraph: what will its **main point** be?

How will you **back up** this point?
- with a reason/evidence?
- with an example from your own experience?
- with further details?

2nd paragraph: what will its **main point** be?

How will you **back up** this point?
- with a reason/evidence?
- with an example from your own experience?
- with further details?

Unit 7
Media today
Lesson 5

Framework Objective
R10: Identify how media texts are tailored to suit their audience, and recognise that audience responses vary
Main text type: Advice

Student Book pages 152–157

Starter

- Brainstorm different advice texts. You could do this orally or build up a spidergram on the board, with 'Advice' in the centre. Ask students what language features these texts may share. Do not comment too much on their responses at this stage: this activity is intended as preparatory.

Introduction

- Read the *mizz* article aloud to the class, ensuring that students understand the terms in the glossary.

Key Reading

- Go through the key features of advice texts, as shown in the text-type box. Check understanding by asking students these questions:
  - *Why is it important for advice texts to be logical?*
  - *What kind of things are we referring to when we say 'design'?*
  - *What is direct address? Give examples.*
- Explain the term 'logical' to the class to inform their analysis of the advice text. Then get students to discuss questions **1** to **3** in pairs. Ask 2 or 3 pairs to feed back their answers and invite the class to comment.
- To extend the work done on direct address, the same pairs can highlight further examples in the copy of the article on **Worksheet 7.5**. They need to be secure on direct address for the 'Key Writing' task later. Invite pairs to present their findings to the class on an OHT version of **Worksheet 7.5**.

Development

Purpose

- Pairs discuss questions **4** and **5** in this section and feed back to the class. If necessary, prompt them for question **5** by indicating that advice texts usually move from giving general information to specific information.

Reading for meaning

- Begin this section by running through the 'Grammar for reading' box on adjectives and connectives. Supply further examples if necessary.
- Ask individuals to think about questions **6** and **7**, and answer them orally. If they point out that there aren't any adjectives in the third sentence, ask them what words create the new mood, for example, *but*, *the fact is* and *risks*.
- Read question **8** with the class and show how the connective signals where the sentence is going. Pairs then discuss the purpose of the connective in another sentence.

Plenary

- Ask students to write down three key features of argument texts, reinforcing these as necessary.

Unit 7 Media today

Worksheet 7.5: Direct address

Highlight at least ten examples of the use of direct address in this advice text below. Write a note in the margin to say what effect each example has on the reader.

Pen Pal Dangers

Thought putting pen to paper was a harmless way of making a new mate? Maybe not – as mizz discovers…

Having a pen pal is a fantastic way to make new mates from different places. By meeting through official school schemes or exchanges where teachers can make sure everything is above board, pen pals can become friends for life. But the fact is, meeting someone via an Internet club or through a magazine does have risks.

Take meeting someone creepy online. It's awful, but you can log off quick sharp. If you've written letters to them, however, that person's got your address, as well as loads of info about you that you've let them in on. It'd be like texting summat really personal to your best mate, then realising someone else had read it instead. So make sure that you get sussed before you start scribbling…

● ● ● ● ● ● ● **Pen Pal Pointers**

First off, don't panic and ring up your pen pal to accuse them of being an impostor. Nearly all people who write'll be genuine, but it's important to follow *mizz*'s safety tips:

 You might get over 100 replies but don't try to juggle too many. Go through 'em with your folks and pick a couple you'd like to be friends with.

 Take your pen pal friendship slowly. There's no need to tell them every little fact about yourself until you know them properly.

 Don't ever give out your address or phone number without checking with your parents first. The best thing to do is get your folks to call the parents of your future pen pal to check everything's cool.

 Make sure that you tell your parents immediately if you read something that makes you feel uncomfortable. You can then tackle the problem together.

And remember – as a *mizz* pen pal, we don't give your address out to any old bod with a fancy stationery set. No personal details appear in the mag. We send you details of your wannabe pen pals and you pick who you want to write to.

From *mizz* magazine

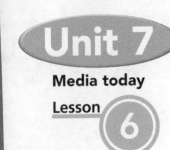

Unit 7
Media today
Lesson 6

Framework Objectives

R13: Identify, using appropriate terminology the way writers of non-fiction match language and organisation to their intentions

Wr17: Write informal advice, anticipating the needs, interests and views of the intended reader

Main text type: Advice

Student Book pages 157–159

Starter

- Write several words and phrases on the board that contain apostrophes of omission. (Discuss apostrophes of possession only if students ask about them.) Ask students what they all have in common. Elicit a class definition of an apostrophe and write it on the board.
- To reinforce the understanding of apostrophes of omission, invite pairs to discuss and complete the activities on **Worksheet 7.6**.

Introduction

Focus on: Informal language

- Discuss whether you use words with apostrophes in formal or informal language. (If necessary, pause to explain these terms.) Emphasise that the nature of the audience is key when it comes to choosing how formal the language is to be. Discuss the audience of *mizz* – what kind of language will they respond to best? Establish why informal language is often more effective for advice texts. (They need to get the audience on-side so that they follow the advice.)
- Read through the section which concentrates on two features of informal language used in the *mizz* text (contracted words and conversational language). Ask pairs to attempt question **9**. Ask 1 or 2 pairs to present their answers to the class, using their table as an OHT. Discuss the final question, which may reveal that some contractions are more acceptable in formal writing than others.
- As an extension to this section, ask students to brainstorm conversational language that used to be in fashion but is no longer, (for example, *trendy* rather than *cool*), to illustrate how quickly the vocabulary of slang changes.

Development

Key Writing

- Read through the section with the class and challenge students to point out the formal language in the 'Further help' box. Model one or two examples on the board of how it could be rewritten so that it is less formal – referring to the 'Remember' bullet points will be crucial here. Revisit the idea of direct address if necessary.
- Once students have ordered the points in the box, ask them to rewrite 'Further help' on their own.

Plenary

- Invite 3 or 4 students to read out their extracts or present them on an OHT to the class. Invite the class to comment on:
  - how well they have made the writing less formal
  - how effective they are as advice texts (or how well the points are organised).

Unit 7 Media today

Worksheet 7.6: Apostrophes

The apostrophe is shaped like a comma in the air, like this: '

One of the things apostrophes are used for is to show where a letter or letters have been missed out of a word. The letters are replaced by an apostrophe. For example:

- I'm going out   (I am → I'm)
- He's had it   (He has → He's)
- They've scored   (They have → They've)

1 Match up each word or phrase on the left with the shortened form on the right. The first one has been done for you.

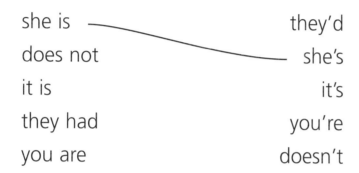

2 In the sentences below, some words have been underlined. Shorten these words by using an apostrophe. Write the shortened form at the end.

a <u>He has</u> got a new pen pal. _____

b <u>It is</u> time to sign out. _____

c <u>Do not</u> go on the Internet now. _____

d <u>They have</u> already logged on. _____

e <u>We had</u> noticed them in the chat room. _____

Impact English Teacher's Resource © HarperCollins Publishers 2005

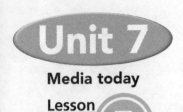

Unit 7
Media today
Lesson 7

Assessment Focuses
- **AF4:** Construct paragraphs and use cohesion within and between paragraphs
- **AF7:** Select appropriate and effective vocabulary
- **Main text type:** Persuasion

Student Book pages 160–161

Starter
- Talk to students about how choosing the right word can make all the difference to the effect of a piece. Hand out copies of **Worksheet 7.7** to pairs to practise choosing appropriate and effective words, depending on the context.

Introduction

Stage 1
- Read through Stage 1. Ask pairs to discuss their celebrities and make a list of at least three qualities for each. Invite 2 or 3 pairs to feed back to the class, to check that everyone is on the right lines.

Stage 2
- Students should work in groups, organised by celebrity if possible, to draft their speech. At this point they need to discuss and agree the best order for their paragraphs to go in.

Development

Stage 3
- Students use their agreed order and work on their own to draft one paragraph for each main point or quality. Go through the example provided to show how each main point needs to be supported by a piece of evidence, a reason, an example or more detail. Guide a group of lower-ability students to share progress, deal with questions and praise effective sentences. At the end of this stage, share good examples of student writing with the class. Model one or two examples on the board.
- Encourage those who have time or ability to practise giving their speech, using the notes from Stage 1 as prompts.

Peer Assessment
- When students have completed their writing, they work in pairs to read each others' draft argument speeches. Write up the text-type features listed below and ask pairs to check if their drafts include them:
  - a series of main points in a logical order
  - main points backed up by a variety of evidence
  - formal but effective language.
- Students then fill in the Peer Assessment Sheet (see page 6) and feed back their findings.
- Students redraft their speech according to suggestions and the redrafting tips on using powerful language, to make the speech more interesting.

Plenary

- Give a copy of **OHT 7.8** (top half only) to each group and get students to annotate the level 3 writing to show how well the student has constructed paragraphs and chosen appropriate and effective vocabulary, and what needs improvement. Then display the whole of **OHT 7.8** and ask for feedback on how to get the level 3 writing up to level 4. Show in the exemplar of level 4 how this can be done. Students can make changes to their own texts in light of this.
- Ask 2 or 3 students to read out or present their speeches, encouraging the class to give constructive criticism on how well they show the features of persuasive argument writing.

Unit 7 Media today

Worksheet 7.7: Suiting words to purpose

1 Many words and phrases in English mean much the same thing. However, there may be a reason why you should use one word rather than another. You have to think about the **purpose** of your writing.

Look at the words in the box on the right.
Which ones would you use to:
a end an email to your mate
b end a letter to your aunt in America
c end a letter asking for a job?

> Lots of love from Jake
> Cheers, Jake XX
> Yours sincerely, Jake Gardiner

Give your reasons here:

a _____

b _____

c _____

2 Some words and phrases are more **effective** than others. Underline the more effective word or phrase in each case below. Then jot down your reason in the space provided.
(All examples are from argument texts.)

a He's a skilful footballer.

He's a good footballer.

Reason: _____

b The restaurant was full of celebrities.

The restaurant was full of important people.

Reason: _____

c His performance captivated the audience.

The audience loved his performance.

Reason: _____

Unit 7 — Media today

OHT 7.8: Peer assessment

Assessment Focuses
- **AF4:** Construct paragraphs and use cohesion within and between paragraphs
- **AF7:** Select appropriate and effective vocabulary

Level 3

Wilkinson spends hours and hours practising his kicking, until he gets it just right, like he did when he dropped that goal in the World Cup final. He is really dedicated and inspires young sportsmen, though he's been through loads of operations on his dodgy shoulder, he's put up with all this hassle with a lot of courage.

Level 4

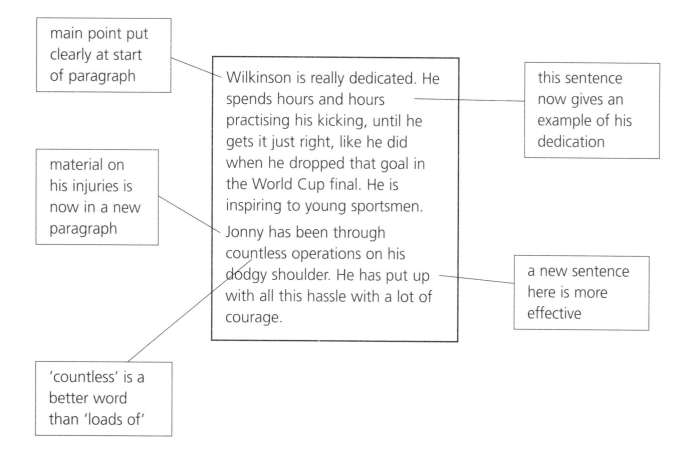

Past lives

Lesson

Framework Objectives

R1: Know how to locate resources for a given task, and find relevant information in them (skimming)

R2: Use appropriate reading strategies to extract particular information (scanning)

Main text type: Recount

Student Book pages 162–166

Starter

- Ask the class if they know the difference between biography and autobiography. Make the difference clear by pointing out that autobiography is written in the first person: 'I'. Then ask students to work out what person biography is written in. Emphasise that both forms of writing are recounts and are written chronologically.

Introduction

Key Reading

- Before reading the Roald Dahl text to students, highlight two other significant features of autobiography – that it is told in the past tense and that it is concerned with memory. Read the text, making sure the students understand the terms in the glossary.
- Then go through the features in the text-type box. Check understanding by asking students these questions:
  - Which pronouns show that the writing is in the first person?
  - Why are recount texts written in the past tense?
  - Can you think of memories from your own life and use time connectives to help sequence them? (For example, When I was five I started school.)
- Then invite students to discuss questions **1** to **4** in pairs. Ask 2 or 3 pairs to feed back their answers and invite the class to comment.
- To extend the work done on time connectives as a tool in ordering events, hand out copies of **Worksheet 8.1** to pairs. Ask them to construct the timeline and to use the appropriate time connectives to complete the sentences.

Purpose

- Ask pairs to discuss which of the options in question **5** explains why they think Roald Dahl wrote about this episode from his childhood. Ask them to consider why they would write their own.

Development

Reading for meaning

- The text is sufficiently accessible for students to find information, so you can introduce the skills of skimming (questions **6** to **8**) and scanning (question **9**). Students should try to remember the difference between the two and use the appropriate terms. They should complete question **8** as soon as possible after hearing the text. (Note which students have difficulty in recalling the order of events and guide them in sequencing the information.)
- When introducing scanning in question **9**, emphasise the usefulness of focusing on key words as an aid to understanding. Initially, students may take some time to extract information. Practice will enable them to build up speed. (See **Worksheet 1.1** for further practice in scanning.)

Plenary

- Recap on the difference between skimming and scanning and the usefulness of both skills. Then elicit the main features of recount texts from the class, reinforcing these as necessary.

Unit 8 Past lives

Worksheet 8.1: Roald Dahl's timeline

Roald Dahl wrote many books for adults and children. The dates below tell you when some of them were published.

Complete the timeline by writing the dates in the correct order.

> *Going Solo* (autobiography 1986)
>
> *Matilda* (1988)
>
> *Boy* (autobiography 1984)
>
> *The BFG* (1982)
>
> *The Gremlins* (1943)
>
> *James and the Giant Peach* (USA 1961, UK 1967)
>
> *Royal Jelly* (short story 1959)

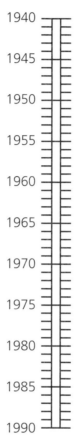

Use the information in the timeline to complete the sentences below. Use the following connectives of time. (You should use one in each sentence.) The first has been done for you as an example.

| before   first   after   next   then   finally   until |

1 <u>The first book</u> Roald Dahl wrote was *The Gremlins*.

2 _____ he wrote stories for adults such as *Royal Jelly*.

3 The _____ book he wrote for children was *James and the Giant Peach* in 1961.

4 *James and the Giant Peach* was not published in the UK _____.

5 *The BFG* was written _____.

6 *Going Solo* was written _____.

7 _____ Roald Dahl wrote *Matilda* in 1988.

Impact English Teacher's Resource © HarperCollinsPublishers 2005

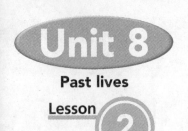

Unit 8
Past lives
Lesson 2

Framework Objectives

S1c: Extend their use and control of complex sentences by deploying subordinate clauses in a variety of positions within the sentence

R14: Recognise how writers' language choices can enhance meaning (emotive vocabulary)

Wr8: Experiment with the visual and sound effects of language, including the use of imagery

Main text type: Recount

Student Book pages 166–168

Starter

- Remind the class of the extract from *Boy*, referring to it as a dramatic episode in Roald Dahl's childhood. Discuss with students the necessity for the writer to maintain the tension (and therefore the reader's interest) throughout paragraph 1 when the doctor performs the procedure.

Introduction

Focus on: Keeping up the tension

- Refer to the example in the Student Book, which studies the construction of the final sentence in paragraph 1. Complete question **10** with the whole class, once they have understood the main point.
- Explain to the class that they can develop their own sentences by adding detail at the end to make them more interesting. Work through the example ('He stared at the deep wound'), pointing out that beginning a phrase with a non-finite verb like 'spurting' (you may wish to refer to it as an '-ing' word) is a useful way of adding extra information.

Development

Key Writing

- The students should use what they have learned about sentence variation and descriptive detail in question **11**. Much of the structure, including the non-finite verb, is provided for them but they must think of vivid descriptions (or images) to add to each sentence.
- Guide a lower-ability group in this initially, sharing ideas for descriptive detail and any sentences that build tension effectively, but students complete the work on their own. When finished, the whole description should read like an episode or event, including time connectives to help sequence events.
- If appropriate, you can introduce **Worksheet 8.2**. In this worksheet sentences begin with the non-finite clause and students need to provide the main clause, which should make sense on its own. Point out that varying sentences will keep up the tension in each case. Point to the main clause in the worksheet example ('he picked up the knife') and again in the Student Book example ('He stared at the deep wound') to reinforce this.

Plenary

- Recap on the main points of the lesson:
  - how tension can be maintained in a sentence by leaving the most important information until the end
  - how sentences can be made more interesting by adding description.
- Invite 3 or 4 students to share their best sentences to illustrate both points. They can choose from their sentences for 'Key Writing' or from **Worksheet 8.2**.

Unit 8 Past lives

Worksheet 8.2: Develop your sentences

These sentences begin with descriptions. Finish each one. (The first has been done for you as an example.)

1 Sweating with fear, <u>he picked up the knife</u>.

2 Screeching to a halt, _____.

3 Flapping its wings, _____.

4 Charging down the road, _____.

5 Tumbling down the hill, _____.

6 Scraping her knee on the gravel, _____.

7 Shouting with anger, _____.

8 Shivering with cold, _____.

Impact English Teacher's Resource © HarperCollinsPublishers 2005

It was long ago

Past lives

Lesson

Framework Objective

R14: Recognise how writers' language choices can enhance meaning (repetition)

Main text type: Poetry

Student Book pages 169–173

Starter

- Students will need to take something of a cultural leap in reading the poem in this section. Explain that it is a classic poem, written and set in the past. As students listen to it, ask them to consider how it differs from their lives and how strongly it conveys time past. The poem offers simple but profound thoughts, accessible to everyone. Check students understand the words in the glossary as you read.

Introduction

Key Reading

- Run through the features in the text-type box. Check understanding by asking students these questions:
  – *Are poems written in lines or sentences?*
  – *Does the poem rhyme or not?*
- Then invite students to discuss questions **1** and **2** in pairs. Ask 2 or 3 pairs to feed back their answers and invite the class to comment. Encourage pairs to refer to evidence from the poem to back up their answers. Point out that even though the poem is in the first person, students should not assume that it is necessarily autobiographical.

Purpose

- Students explore how the poem makes them feel in questions **3** and **4**. Focus on the final line, 'Then I grew up you see', which brings the reader back to the present abruptly, with a sense of loss. While the students may not be able to articulate this, they should detect the sadness in the last line.

Development

Reading for meaning

- Discuss the effect of repetition in the poem with the students. Begin by looking at the words 'I remember'. Both the meaning of these words and their repetition emphasise the fact that this is a memory, as does, 'It was long ago'. Students will return to find other examples of repetition in question **6**.
- Next look at the simple rhyme pattern, showing students how it works in question **5**: abc is repeated throughout but is broken regularly in the third, sixth, ninth and twelfth verses with abb.
- Point out that all these features of the poem work together to emphasise the importance of the key lines 'I remember'/'It was long ago' and the feeling produced.
- Students can extend this work on the effect of repetition in **Worksheet 8.3**. Groups analyse three verses from *The Rime of the Ancient Mariner*, which also contains several examples of repetition. They then report their findings to the class.

Plenary

- Recap the main points of the lesson, eliciting from students, if possible, how repetition can bring out the central idea in a poem and evoke a feeling – in this case, sadness and the importance of memory.

Unit 8 Past lives

Worksheet 8.3: The effect of repetition

In *The Rime of the Ancient Mariner*, a sailor returns from sea with a strange tale. He has killed an albatross – a bird that usually brings good luck. His act, it seems, has cursed the ship.

In these verses the heat is intense. There is no wind to drive the sails and no fresh water to drink.

> *From*
> **'The Rime of the Ancient Mariner'**
>
> All in a hot and copper sky,
> The bloody Sun, at noon,
> Right up above the mast did stand,
> No bigger than the Moon.
>
> Day after day, day after day,
> We stuck, nor breath nor motion; — no wind to drive the ship
> As idle as a painted ship
> Upon a painted ocean.
>
> Water, water, every where,
> And all the boards did shrink;
> Water, water, every where,
> Nor any drop to drink.
>
> by Samuel Taylor Coleridge

1 How did the poem make you feel?

Circle more than one of the following if you wish.

worried   scared   thoughtful   want to know what happens

2 What is repeated in these verses? How many examples can you find?

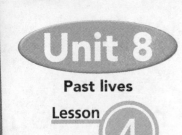

Unit 8
Past lives
Lesson 4

Framework Objective
Wr8: Experiment with the sound effects of language, including the use of rhythm and rhyme
Main text type: Poetry

Student Book pages 173–175

Starter

- Open the lesson with a discussion of rhythm and its presence all around us. Ask students to think of examples (*rhythm of music, of the heart, of a train, of the tides*).

Introduction

Focus on: Rhythm

- Ensure students understand what a syllable is. If they are uncertain, explain by referring to the example 're-mem-ber' in the Student Book. Point out that all speech has rhythm and refer to 're-mem-ber' again to note the difference between stressed and unstressed syllables. Emphasise that many words in English are heavily accented. Students then complete question **7** in pairs.
- To extend this work, students can complete **Worksheet 8.4**, which looks in greater detail at stress patterns in individual words. A regional dialect can make a difference to some stress patterns and you may wish to take this into account.
- In question **8** students examine the strong rhythm present in the poem, referring to verse 4. Draw parallels with the rhythm of poetry and the 'beat' of music. Pairs can tap out the beat of the line, 'She seemed the oldest thing I can remember,' but should feel the rhythm without tapping out the beat in the next example. They then compare this with another verse in the poem to establish that the rhythm is regular in question **9**. When pairs have established the nature of the poem's rhythm, emphasise that this regularity is another example of repetition (again serving to reinforce the importance of the memory in the poem).

Development

Key Writing

- For question **11** students should look again at their idea for their special memory from **Lesson 2**, ('Key Writing', page 175) and use this to create a poem of three rhyming couplets. While most students will be able to rhyme, they may find it difficult to do so convincingly. Encourage them to create a range of five or six rhyming couplets and then to discard those that do not work. Rhyming words are supplied to help them. Students should also try to keep the rhythm of each line the same.

Plenary

- Elicit from students what a syllable is and some examples of stressed and unstressed syllables. Recap on the rhythmic pattern of *It was Long Ago* and the effect of this repetition. Invite 2 or 3 students to read out their couplets and ask the class to comment on the effectiveness of the rhyme and rhythm.

Unit 8 Past lives

Worksheet 8.4: Where's the beat?

1 First split the words below into syllables. The first example has been done for you.

2 Underline the syllable that is stressed (where the beat falls). If you are not sure, try stressing different syllables and see which does not sound right.

3 In which word do the syllables have the same stress?

Words	Syllables and stress
again	a/gain
couplet	
music	
poetry	
regular	
repeating	
hip-hop	
fantastic	

Impact English Teacher's Resource © HarperCollinsPublishers 2005

Unit 8
Past lives
Lesson 5

Framework Objectives

R8: Infer and deduce meanings using evidence in the text, identifying where and how meanings are implied

Wr19: Write reflectively about a text, taking account of the needs of others who might read it

Main text type: Analysis

Student Book pages 176–180

Starter

- Introduce the word 'analysis' and explain its meaning by referring to an everyday example (for example, when we study a football team's potential for the season). Emphasise that students weigh up (analyse) evidence regularly, deciding what is reliable, perhaps without realising it. Point out that students can learn to observe closely and ask the right questions to test the evidence even in those areas where knowledge is limited. Explain that they do this in a range of subjects, such as Science and History.

Introduction

- The section looks at historical sources and their reliability. Students will almost certainly have studied source material in History and read commentaries about it. The difference will be in the tone of the King Arthur text, which is less serious than most textbooks.

Key Reading

- Read the text and refer to the sources before running through the features in the text-type box. Check understanding by asking students these questions:
  - *Why is evidence used for each main point?*
  - *Which tense is mainly used in an analysis text?*
  - *Which two types of connective help examine source material?*
- Then invite students to discuss questions **1** to **4** in pairs. Ask 2 or 3 pairs to feed back their answers and invite the class to comment. Explain how and why the present and past tenses are used once students have located examples in questions **3** and **4**.

Purpose

- Questions **5** and **6** should be worked on in pairs so that students look closely at the nature of the four sources chosen and find the main purpose of the text.

Development

Reading for meaning

- Work through questions **7** to **10** with the class. Elicit from students how the layout with its subheadings – often posed as questions – helps to break up the analysis. Explain that when complex information is staged, the reader can follow ideas more easily. Refer to the use of bullet points and questions. Discuss the way in which the text shows the unreliability of the evidence in questions **8** and **9**, and point out that asking the right questions helps us with problem-solving. Detailed discussion of sources 1 and 4 will help prepare students for the 'Key Speaking and Listening' task.
- To extend work on asking the right questions, students work in pairs to complete **Worksheet 8.5**. This involves a conversation in which only the answers are given and students supply the correct question. It also involves a puzzle for students to solve. Point to the way in which the questions help deduce the answer. (In this case, the questions relate to the object's function, what it cannot do and the material it is made of. The answer is 'kettle'.)
- Return to the text in question **10** to look at the humorous tone adopted by the writer and ask pairs to find two examples of this.

Plenary

- Ask pairs to feed back on question **10** and explore how the chosen tone makes the analysis more interesting or effective.
- Run through the main points of the lesson – that is, what an analysis is, presenting points clearly in the text, looking at evidence by observing closely and asking the right questions.

Unit 8 Past lives

Worksheet 8.5: Question setting

Below is a conversation between two students about an object used in the kitchen. One of them is trying to guess what the object is by asking questions. Work out what questions he asks by looking at the answers you have been given. The first has been done for you.

Is it used in cooking ?

Yes, it is used in cooking.

_____?

No, you can't keep food in it.

_____?

Yes, it will hold liquid.

_____?

No, it isn't made of china.

_____?

Yes, it is made of metal.

_____?

No, you can't keep it in a fridge.

_____?

No, you can't use it in an oven.

_____?

You can use some kinds on the hob of a cooker, but not others.

_____?

It can be electrical, but it doesn't have to be.

_____?

Yes, it can heat something.

Can you guess what it is? _____

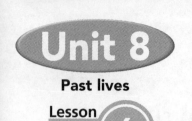

Unit 8
Past lives
Lesson 6

Framework Objectives

W20: Expand the range of link words and phrases used to signpost texts, including links of cause

R8: Infer and deduce meanings using evidence in the text, identifying where and how meanings are implied

S&L1: Use talk as a tool for clarifying ideas

Main text type: Analysis

Student Book pages 181–182

Starter

- Ask students if they can recall the main features of an analysis text. Then introduce the idea that connectives can help to express complicated ideas. Refer back to the example in the text-type box to explain that connectives of cause and effect help to link the reason for something happening with what happens.

Introduction

Focus on: Using connectives of cause, effect and contrast

- Run through the worked sentences from the text which give concrete examples of causal relationships, focusing on the connectives 'so' and 'because'. Explain that the link between cause and effect can be expressed in more than one way.
- Then ask students to complete question **11**, which focuses on the difference in meaning between 'so' and 'because', and question **12**, where they select the right causal connective to link the two sentences. Please note that the adverb 'so' can be used to join parts of a sentence; strictly speaking, in this context, it is a conjunction. However, it can also link sentences in a paragraph (where it would be regarded as a connective). See **Worksheet 8.6**.
- Students then study how connectives that contrast views are used in the text. In question **13**, they work with connectives that analyse contrasting views of a single source.
- Students can extend this work by completing **Worksheet 8.6**, which reinforces the usefulness of connectives.

Development

Key Speaking and Listening

- For question **14**, small groups discuss in an organised way whether King Arthur existed or not and why the legend has survived so long. Stress that they can draw on their knowledge of the sources 1 to 4 from the 'Reading for meaning' section. Encourage them to refer closely to the text and to use the connectives 'so' or 'because' to express causal relationships and 'but' to show contrasting views.
- Groups then evaluate how well they worked together and expressed their views, using the bullets provided.

Plenary

- Invite 2 or 3 group representatives to feed back the main points of their evaluation of their group discussion, encouraging them to use the language of analysis.

Unit 8 Past lives

Worksheet 8.6: Using connectives

1 Complete these sentences about the sources you have been studying.

2 Underline in red the connectives that show cause and effect in each sentence.

Firstly, the history book De Excidio Britanniae mentions an important soldier but

Secondly, the Modena Cathedral Carving of 1120 probably pictures 'Arthur of Britannia' because

Thirdly, the main problem with the Historia Regum Britanniae (a 12th century text) is that

Lastly, Arthur's grave at Glastonbury seems convincing because

However, the monks

So, we can say that it is most likely that King Arthur

Past lives

Assessment Focus

AF3: Organise and present whole texts effectively, sequencing and structuring information, ideas and events

Main text type: Analysis

Student Book pages 183–185

Starter

- Ask students to write down three main features of analysis texts, then feed back to the class. Explain the students' role as historians and the purpose of the assignment as outlined. Emphasise that they need to write in clear stages and study the evidence, which you then turn to. Point to the information supplied about the source (i.e. the writer, text and when it was written). Inform students that Henry Mayhew recorded the words of the poor 'from the lips of the people themselves'. Read the extract to the class, explaining that being a mud-lark was a way of earning a living.

Introduction

Stage 1

- Students make notes on the list of questions, which will help them find appropriate information in the source. Either answer all questions with the class or ask students to work in groups, each completing the answers to questions under 'Information' and then appointing someone to report back so you can clarify any problems.

Stage 2

- Questions under 'The quality of evidence' are answered with the class. Note students' comments on the board and fill in any additional information (for example, a weakness is the brevity of the extract).

Development

Stage 3

- Students use the work they have done, along with the writing frame (**Worksheet 8.7**) and advice in the Student Book, to write their two-paragraph analysis.
- Remind students again that they will need to set out their ideas clearly so that the reader can follow the main points. Model how the writing frame helps students with paragraphing and cohesion by using connectives to link paragraphs.

Peer Assessment

- When students have completed their writing, they work in pairs to read each others' drafts. Write up the text-type features listed below and ask pairs to check if their drafts include them:
  - use of present tense for analysis/past tense for past events
  - use of evidence to back up main points
  - connectives of cause and contrast to bring out reasons and views.
- Students then fill in the Peer Assessment Sheet (see page 6) and feed back their findings.
- Students redraft according to suggestions.

Plenary

- Give a copy of **OHT 8.8** (top half only) to groups and get students to annotate the level 3 writing to show how well the student has used causal connectives, especially to contrast or qualify, and what needs improvement. Then display the whole of **OHT 8.8** and ask for feedback on how to get the level 3 writing up to level 4. Show in the exemplar of level 4 how it can be done.

Challenge

- Help students to redraft their analyses, by lengthening sentence and varying their structure. See examples given in the Student Book.
- Ask 2 or 3 students to read their texts to the class and ask for constructive criticism from the other students.

Unit 8 Past lives

Worksheet 8.7: Writing up your notes

Use this writing frame to help you write your Unit 8 Assignment.

Paragraph 1

Source A is written evidence that comes from…

_____

It was…

_____

It tells us…

_____

There is…

_____

Think of two more sentences to add.

_____

_____

Paragraph 2

Overall I think that…

_____

because…

_____

But…

_____

Think of two more sentences to add.

_____

_____

Unit 8 Past lives

OHT 8.8: Peer assessment

Assessment Focus

AF3: Organise and present whole texts effectively, sequencing and structuring information, ideas and events

Level 3

Source A is written evidence. It comes from, 'London Labour and the London Poor', by Henry Mayhew. It was written in 1861 and tells us about the mud-lark. He was someone who searched in the mud on the riverbank. He searched for things to sell.

There is an interview with a mud-lark in the book. The words are the words he spoke. So this means we can trust what the writer tells us.

Level 4

longer sentence tells us about the source

> Source A is written evidence that comes from 'London Labour and the London Poor' by Henry Mayhew. It was written in 1861 and tells us about the life of a mud-lark. This was someone who searched in the mud on the riverbank for objects to sell.
>
> There is an interview with a mud-lark included. The words are his. So the writer's information is reliable.
>
> Overall, I think that this is useful evidence because it tells us about children's lives. However, the paragraph is short. So I think we should look for more evidence to back this up.

more suitable connective to qualify the point

one sentence instead of two makes the point

connective tells us the evidence is useful

extra paragraph gives the writer's personal view

Impact English Teacher's Resource © HarperCollins*Publishers* 2005

Sporting challenge

Lesson 1

Framework Objectives
W6: Revise, consolidate and secure the use of the possessive apostrophe
S13b: Revise the stylistic conventions of recount texts
Main text type: Recount

Student Book pages 186–190

Starter

- Recap on the use of the possessive apostrophe with the class by giving them this example from the Ellen MacArthur text (before they read it):
  Auntie Thea's sloop (the sloop – a boat – belonging to Auntie Thea)
  Then ask the students to put in apostrophes for:
  – *Ellens grandmother*
  – *girls things* (two possibilities).

Introduction

Key Reading

- Read the website text aloud to the class, checking that any difficult glossary words are understood. Check that students are clear about what 'autobiography' means.
- Go through the key text-type features of recounts, as shown in the text-type box on page 188. Check students' understanding by asking them to:
  – *offer the present tense alternative to 'sailed'* (sails or is sailing)
  – *briefly recount what they did that morning in time order* (got up, then had breakfast…)
  – *think of any other connectives to do with time* ('later', 'firstly', 'next', 'afterwards', 'in the end', 'lastly', 'then').
- Use **OHT 9.1** to reinforce these points, asking the class to suggest the correct order. (Answer: D, A, G, C, E, F, B, J, H, I.) The class can also highlight connectives of time before completing questions **1** to **4** as a shared exercise.

Purpose

- Work through question **5** with the students, discussing the options. Ask them to explain their choice.

Development

Reading for meaning

- Discuss with the class how we decide what the main focus of a text is (i.e. what it is about), by looking at titles, who is mentioned most, etc. Then answer question **6**. Ensure the class is clear about subheadings and their functions before asking them to complete questions **7**, **8** and **9** on their own, writing their answers down.

Plenary

- Review and revise the three key elements of recount texts by asking the students to correct this sentence: *I will be having my breakfast then getting up after leaving for school.*

Unit 9 Sporting challenge

OHT 9.1: Time sequence

Put these sentences about an African safari in the correct order.

A
About half an hour later we gathered round the fire for breakfast.

B
We photographed them for a second time until they disappeared.

C
At midday we stopped to watch a herd of rhinos go by.

D
We woke at dawn, about 6am.

E
We took pictures in case we didn't see them again.

F
Later, we saw the rhinos once more.

G
By 10am we had packed our tents away.

H
Then the jeeps came to a halt and we made camp for the evening.

I
Soon, we were all sitting round the fire for our evening meal.

J
By late afternoon, we were all hot and tired.

Ellen MacArthur's inspiration

 **Sporting challenge**

Lesson

Framework Objectives

R1: Know how to locate resources for a given task, and find relevant information in them (key words)

R4: Make brief, clearly organised notes of key points for later use

Main text type: Recount

Student Book pages 190–191

Starter

- Ask students to suggest situations in which the skill of note-making would be useful (for example: *phone calls, directions, researching information in a book for an essay, science lessons*). Ask them what they understand 'making notes' to mean.

Introduction

Focus on: Finding information and making clear notes

- Work through the section, including question **10**, as a whole class. Draw attention to the fact that finding information is dependent on being clear about what it is you are looking for. In other words, the first piece of information, about Ellen's nan, would not be useful in the article – students will be writing about a <u>sports person</u> who is inspiring (in this case, Ellen).
- Then take the class through the sequence of how to make notes in the way described on page 191 by cutting out unnecessary information and simplifying. When they have completed work on question **11**, give out **Worksheet 9.2** and ask students to work through it in pairs. Share answers and praise those who have got their notes into the most succinct form.

Development

Key Writing

- Students attempt question **12** on their own, putting into practice their note-making skills. Identify and work with those students who continue to write out in full sentences, or who simply copy out from the passage.
- More confident students could perhaps turn their notes back into prose, by writing a paragraph of approximately 35–45 words in which they say why Ellen is inspiring. They could start: *Ellen is an inspiring person because she…*

Plenary

- Recap on what has been covered in this section by asking students to recall the main features of the recount text, and also the key skills involved in making simple notes. If time allows, end with a quick game using the script below, in which you pretend to make a phone call to them from which they must note the key information:

    Hi, it's Jo. Is everything ok? Yeah, I had a great journey so I'll be back sooner than I thought. Can Dad pick me up from the bus station at about 11.30 tomorrow morning? Not Wednesday as we arranged, but Tuesday. Oh, by the way, tell Mum I've got that CD she liked. See ya!

- For homework, students could research the life of a celebrity they like and write brief notes (i.e. up to ten bullet points) on his or her main achievements.

Unit 9 Sporting challenge

Worksheet 9.2: Note-making

Turn this short extract into simple notes. Check what you need to note down first.

> **RATS**
> The Norwegian Rat is sometimes known as the Brown Rat. It is quite large and can be found living all over the world. It has a scaly tail. It is almost hairless. It has a brownish grey back and is white underneath. It is a good swimmer and often lives near water.

Make notes on what the Norwegian Rat looks like.

Your notes

Impact English Teacher's Resource © HarperCollins Publishers 2005

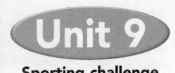 

Sporting challenge

Lesson 3

Framework Objectives	
S15:	Vary the formality of language in speech and writing to suit different circumstances
R1:	Know how to locate resources for a given task, and find relevant information in them (key words)
Main text type: Narrative	

Student Book pages 192–197

Starter

- Ask students to consider the different ways, 'I'm so glad you came!' could be said, for example sarcastically, genuinely delighted, falsely. Make the point that in written speech, details of gestures (someone nodding their head, crossing their arms or reaching out to touch someone else) and tone of voice need to be included – gestures that in spoken conversation make things clearer.
- Then discuss what the writer actually does to convey Jules' feelings (adds 'yelled', and tells us that Jules gives Jess a hug). Similarly, the formality of language changes depending on the context. For example, in a job application you would not write, 'I'm well up for this job – it's totally wicked', but you might write, 'I am very pleased to have this opportunity'.

Introduction

Key Reading

- Read the *Bend it like Beckham* extract with the students, checking that difficult glossary words are understood.
- Go through the key text-type features of narratives, as listed on page 194. Point out that although the overall narrative structure of the novel/film fits the classic structure, every chapter is full of problems and complications – and dramatic moments. Even in this extract, there are several potential problems. Check understanding by asking students:
  - *What features of narrative structure can they find in this extract?*
  - *Are there any potential problems in the extract?* (Will Jules be friends with her? Will the other team score from the free kick? Will the other team win?)
  - *Are the problems resolved?* (Yes: Jules is still her friend, the other team doesn't score again, Jules scores an equaliser.)
- Then go through questions **1** to **3** with the class, to ensure that the features of the text type are embedded.

Purpose

- Ask students to suggest what the effect is of telling us Jess's team are "1–0 down" (creates suspense).

Development

Reading for meaning

- Use this section to revisit and revise the idea of looking for key information, which was introduced when looking at the previous text on Ellen MacArthur. Answer questions **4a** and **4b** as a class, using what has been learned, and then distribute **Worksheet 9.3**. Show students how to annotate the two questions and highlight the key words before answering. Finish by asking students to answer questions **5** and **6** in pairs, justifying their answers.

Plenary

- Finish by asking students to recall how a typical episode of a soap might have an overall problem (such as a secret one character has from another), but is also full of individual problems (that character almost giving the secret away, being asked the truth by another, etc.). Students might be asked to watch an episode and make notes on the complications (big and small) a character faces.

Unit 9 Sporting challenge

Worksheet 9.3: Finding information

Find the key words in questions c) and d) from page 196 in your Student Book and make notes about the clues they give you. Then find the answers to the questions in the text.

c Who catches the ball from the QPR free kick?

> They were only just outside the penalty area, and this was their chance to grab another goal. I could feel the blood rushing in my ears as I watched the player run up to take it. Being two down would be no joke. But the ball sailed over the top of the wall, and Charlie caught it safely.

d How did Jules fool the QPR defence?

> I watched as Mel passed the ball to Jules while we ran from the centre into the QPR half. I knew what Jules was going to do - and she did it. She let the ball roll through her legs to me, completely fooling the QPR defence. I picked it up quickly behind her…

Impact English Teacher's Resource © HarperCollinsPublishers 2005

Unit 9
Sporting challenge
Lesson 4

Framework Objectives

S7: Use speech punctuation accurately to integrate speech into larger sentences

Wr5: Structure a story with a complication

Main text type: Narrative

Student Book pages 197–198

Starter

- Students can talk about the soap episode they watched for the **Lesson 3** Plenary homework, and the extent to which it depended on complications and problems for the main characters. When do students think the climax will come? Perhaps it happened in that episode. How do soaps differ from most films or novels? (They have multiple storylines with several climaxes at key moments through the year – students may know when these are, such as Christmas or New Year.)

Introduction

Focus on: How to punctuate speech in longer sentences

- Go through page 197 of the Student Book, ensuring that students are clear about the key conventions of writing speech. Ask them to complete question **7** and then go through the answer with them. Then use **OHT 9.4** to demonstrate and share their knowledge. Note that they do not have to separate the speech into new lines as this has been done for them. A suggested answer is:

   "It's great to see you," Steve said.
   "Who's that gorgeous guy over there?" she asked.
   "How should I know?" he replied.
   "It's your brother, isn't it?" Tina said.
   "No."
   "It is!"
   "I can't believe you fancy him!" Steve yelled.

Development

Key Writing

- Discuss question **8** with the class, including the example. Ask the students to think of what else Jess might want to say to Jules after the game. Students consolidate their knowledge of speech punctuation by writing individual responses to the question, composing a conversation and punctuating the speech correctly.

Plenary

- Share the responses that individuals make, selecting 1 or 2 students to write on the board what they have written, and then ask the remainder of the class to decide if the conventions of speech have been applied correctly. For homework, some students could complete or add to Jess and Jules' dialogue.

Unit 9 Sporting challenge

OHT 9.4: Speech punctuation

It's great to see you Steve said

Who's that gorgeous guy over there she asked

How should I know he replied

It's your brother isn't it Tina said

No

It is

I can't believe you fancy him Steve yelled

Top bike techniques

Sporting challenge

Lesson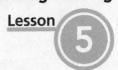

Framework Objective

S13d: Revise the stylistic conventions of instruction texts
Main text type: Instruction

Student Book pages 199–204

Starter

- Write these instructions on the board:
  First, position the ball. Then take aim. Keep your head down. Finally, hit the ball with the inside of your foot to make it curl.
  Ask students: *What sort of text is this? How do you know?*

Introduction

- Now read the biking text with the students, checking that difficult glossary words are understood.

Key Reading

- Go through the key features of instruction texts as in the text-type box on page 201. Check understanding by asking students:
  – *Does the design of the extract makes it easy to follow?*
  – *Find one example of a time connective.*
  – *What is a verb?*
- Make the link between the example in the Starter and the features of the text. Work through questions **1** to **3** to embed the text-type features. Point out that in most instruction texts, the imperative verbs tend to be verbs of action, but that commands such as 'Note that...' ,'Take care to...', or 'Think before you...' are not physical actions that we can see, but states of mind.

Purpose

- Write the sentence: 'To reduce the weight on the front wheel, move your weight backwards' on the board. Ask students what difference this makes from the original (it puts the effect first, and makes the command less strong).
- Go through question **4** with the students to demonstrate the other ways a command can be made less forceful. Then they should say the lines aloud to help them decide on the answer to question **5**.

Development

Reading for meaning

- Discuss students' answers to question **6**. Do they agree that the subheadings make the text easier to follow? Then work through question **7** ensuring they are aware how important the 'preciseness' of the instruction is – and the contribution that adverbs and prepositions (if you wish to discuss these) make to the text. Run through the explanations on **OHT 9.5** to help students.

Plenary

- Write the instructions below on the board and ask students to edit them to make them specific, easy to follow and clearly sequenced. Remind them of the key features of instruction texts.
  It'd be quite good if your mum or dad, or someone, picked you up at about 3 or 4, or maybe 5 o'clock. You might like to arrive in the morning some time. Oh yeah, food for lunch would be useful. You'll need to bring your own BMX.

Impact English Teacher's Resource © HarperCollinsPublishers 2005

Unit 9 Sporting challenge

OHT 9.5: Adverbs

An adverb is a word that provides more information about a verb, an adjective, or even another adverb.

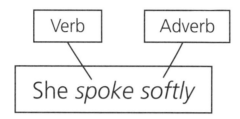

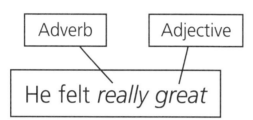

You might think 'really' goes with the verb 'felt', but it doesn't. It is telling us 'how great' so it is providing more information about the adjective ('great').

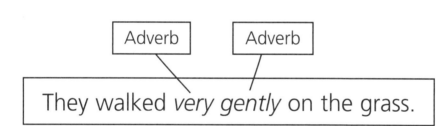

Here, 'gently' adds more information to 'how they walked'. 'Very' tells us 'how gently'.

ADVERBS can tell us about:
- manner (the way something is done) – 'gently'
- degree/amount (how much/great, etc.) – 'very', 'quite'
- place (where) – 'there'
- movement – 'forwards'
- time – 'soon', 'yesterday'

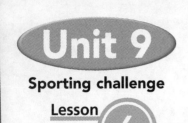

Framework Objectives

Wr13: Give instructions and directions which are specific, easy to follow and clearly sequenced

S&L10: Identify and report the main points emerging from discussion

Main text type: Instruction

Student Book pages 204–205

Starter

- Revise verbs and adverbs by inviting students to sort these words into three columns or lists. Ones they're not sure of can then be explored, or left to return to at a suitable time.
  Words to sort:

think	nasty	hungrily	nastily	move	hungry
speak	fearfully	gently	swiftly	forwards	push

  Headings:
   Verbs   *Adverbs*   *Others* (probably adjectives)

- You may wish to point out that some adverbs work best with actions rather than states (that is, it is difficult to 'feel nastily'). Point out, however, that just because an adverb doesn't fit with a verb doesn't mean its not an adverb!

Introduction

Focus on: Instructions that are easy to follow

- This develops the work in **Lesson 5**, showing that instructions are often accompanied by effects or reasons. These explain *why* the instruction is being given and make it more likely that the instruction will be taken seriously by the person it is being given to.
- Work through question **8**, asking students to suggest endings (humorous if they wish) for the sentence starters.

Development

Key Writing

- Ask the students to work in groups of 4 to 6. Introduce the task as explained in the Student Book, and go through the various points with the class. Give out **Worksheet 9.6** and make sure each group understands what they have to do (to write down on the sheet what makes a good set of instructions, NOT the instructions themselves). They will all need to agree on what makes a good set of instructions. Then they can write down on a separate sheet the instructions themselves.
- Listen in on groups as they discuss the task, and ask individuals what they have agreed 'good instructions' are, and look at the instructions they come up with.

Plenary

- Ask 1 member of each group to report back, telling the rest of the class what they think makes a good set of instructions, and what instructions they came up with. The rest of the class evaluates whether these are good instructions, or need improvement.
- Look at each group's written work and feed back with any comments.

Unit 9 Sporting challenge

Worksheet 9.6: Discussion time

1 Agree as a group what makes a good set of instructions, and list your ideas below.

Good instructions are:

1 *clear and ...*

2

3

4

2 Now discuss the instructions you need to send out to parents and make a list of them on a separate sheet.

Unit 9
Sporting challenge
Lesson 7

Assessment Focuses

AF3: Organise and present whole texts effectively, sequencing and structuring information, ideas and events

AF6: Write with technical accuracy of syntax and punctuation in phrases, clauses and sentences

Main text type: Recount

Student Book pages 206–207

Starter

- Recap on the key text-type features of a recount text, as covered on page 188.

Introduction

Stage 1
- Read through the notes in Stage 1 with the students.

Stage 2
- Work together to complete this stage. Depending on ability level, you might like to ask students to allocate the subheadings on their own, or to conduct guided group work.

Development

Stage 3
- Model the 'Early life' section with students, as shown in the Student Book, drawing attention to the way the notes are transformed into sentences through:
  - adding verbs to create full sentences (*was* born)
  - adding connectives to link pieces of information (*and*)
  - adding pronouns and articles (<u>the</u> 1998 World Cup, <u>they</u> met).
- Discuss with the students how this fairly basic recount could be made more interesting (by adding further detail). For example, start with the following sentence:
  Thierry Henry was born 17 August 1977. He signed for First Division Monaco in 1990.
  Show how it can be improved by using noun phrases and connectives to include more detail on his age, for example:
  Thierry Henry was born 17 August 1977 and signed for First Division Monaco in 1990, at the early age of 13.
  Then add further clauses (with more noun phrases):
  Thierry Henry was born 17 August 1977 and signed for the respected First Division club Monaco in 1990, at the early age of 13.
- Look at **OHT 9.7**. First, highlight the basic features of recounts in the top sample (past tense – grew up; time connective – *before*; chronological order – *birth, then school*). Then ask students to talk about how the second sample has improved on the basic recount (adding words to make full sentences, using time connectives to link events, adding more details to make it more interesting, etc.).
- Point out that the samples are written in the first person, but that their assignment will be written in the third person. Then students can begin their own sports reporter assignment.

Peer Assessment

- When students have completed their writing, they work in pairs and read each others' draft narratives. Write up the text-type features listed below and ask pairs to check if their drafts include them:
  - use of the past tense
  - describes events in time order (chronological order)
  - use of time connectives (words that tell us the order of events).
- They then fill in the Peer Assessment Sheet (see page 6) and feed back their findings.
- Students redraft according to suggestions.

Plenary

- Give a copy of **OHT 9.8** (top half only) to each group and get students to annotate the level 3 writing to show how well the student has structured their text and used punctuation, and what needs improvement. Then display the whole of **OHT 9.8** and ask for feedback on how to get the level 3 writing up to level 4. Show in the exemplar of level 4 how it can be done.
- Share some of the completed profiles. Ask students to consider if they have sufficiently 'fleshed-out' the original notes to make them work as an interesting profile. If not, work together to redraft, adding and altering in order to make the text work as a recount.

Unit 9 Sporting challenge

OHT 9.7: Recount samples

Sample One

> I was born in 1973 in Ethiopia. I was the eighth of five brothers and four sisters. I grew up in a hut. This was home to the eleven members of my family. A normal day started at six. My brothers and sisters and I had to prepare everything before school started. School was over 10km away and we had to make our way through forests, gorges, roads and a river. It was because of this journey that I began to run.
>
> *Haile Gebrsellasie, runner*

Sample Two

> I was born in 1973 in the Ethiopian countryside, 175km from the capital Addis Ababa. I was the eighth of five brothers and four sisters, and grew up in a small hut known as a tucal, a one-room home consisting of mud and wood walls and a straw roof. This was home to the eleven members of my family. A normal day started at six in the morning. My brothers and sisters and I had to prepare everything before school started at eight. School was over 10km away and we had to make our way through forests, gorges, muddy roads and a river. It was because of this journey that I began to run.
>
> *Haile Gebrsellasie, double Olympic champion, and world record-holding runner*

Unit 9 Sporting challenge

OHT 9.8: Peer assessment

Assessment Focuses

AF3: Organise and present whole texts effectively, sequencing and structuring information, ideas and events

AF6: Write with technical accuracy of syntax and punctuation in phrases, clauses and sentences

Level 3

Thierry Henry was born in Paris, France in August 1977. He was brought up in a poor suburb of Paris. He had a lot of support from his family.

He signed for First Division Monaco under manager Arsene Wenger aged 13 he played his first professional game for Monaco aged 17.

Level 4

Nouns expanded with more detail

Soccer star, Thierry Henry was born in Paris, France in August 1977 and was brought up in a poor suburb of Paris. He had a lot of support from his family. This helped him do well at the game he loved.

Then, at the age of 13, he was signed by the respected French First Division club Monaco by manager Arsene Wenger, and played his first professional game for them aged only 17.

Link words/connectives added

More detail given, sentences expanded

Punctuation added

Impact English Teacher's Resource © HarperCollinsPublishers 2005